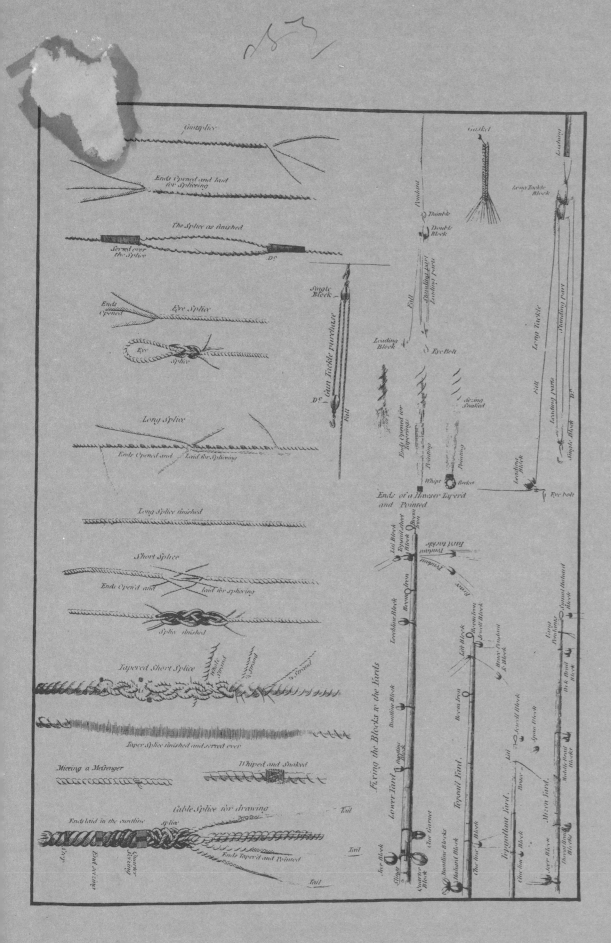

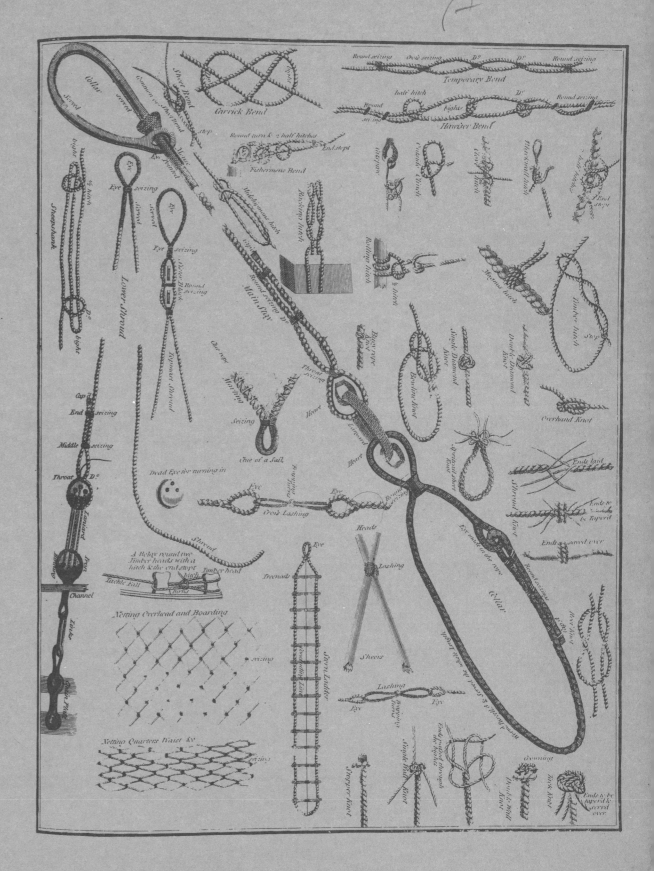

Publd. as the Act directs, Feb. 14. 1794. for D. Steel, Bookseller, Tower Hill.

Publd. as the Act directs, Feb. 14. 1794. for D. Steel, Bookseller, Tower Hill.

THE STORY OF
YACHTING

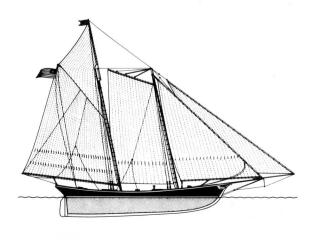

YACHT PAINTIN'S

'Some likes paintin's o' women,' said Bill, 'an' some likes 'orses best,'
As he fitted a pair of fancy shackles on his old sea chest,
'But I likes paintin's o' yachts,' said he, 'an' you can keep the rest.

'An' if I was a ruddy millionaire with dollars to burn that way,
Instead of a dead broke sailorman as never saves his pay,
I'd go to some big paintin' guy, an' this is what I'd say:

'"Paint me the old *America*," I'd say, "or the death of the *Valkyrie*,
Or the *Waterwitch* as I sailed in once in my young days at sea,
Shipshape and Bristol fashion, too, as a great yacht ought to be . . .

'"An' you might do 'er outward bound, with a sky full o' clouds,
An' the dinghy just droppin' astern, an' gulls flyin' in crowds,
An' the decks shiny-wet with rain, an' the wind shakin' the shrouds . . .

'"Or else racin' up the Channel with a fierce sou'wester blowin',
Storm sails set aloft an' alow, an' a hoist o' flags showin',
An' a white bone between her teeth so's you can see she's goin' . . .

'"Or you might do 'er off Cape Horn, in the cold latitudes yonder,
With 'er smooth deck a smother o' white, an' her lee rail dippin' under,
An' the big greybeards racin' by an' breakin' aboard like thunder . . .

'"An' I don't want no dabs o' paint as you can't tell what they are,
Whether they're shadders, or feller's faces, or blocks, or blobs o' tar,
But I want gear as looks like gear, an' a spar that's like a spar.

'"An' I don't care if it's North or South, the Trades or the Baltic sea,
Shortened down or everything set – close-hauled or runnin' free –
You paint me a yacht as is like a yacht . . . an' that'll do for me!"'

THE STORY OF
YACHTING

PAINTINGS BY Tim Thompson
WRITTEN BY Ranulf Rayner

W. W. NORTON & COMPANY
New York   London

To my Mother, who once admitted to the press
when her sons were rescued from their sinking
yacht by two lifeboats, 'Yes, I was worried –
that they might catch a cold.'

A donation from the proceeds of this book will be
given to the Royal National Lifeboat Institution

British Library Cataloguing in Publication Data
Rayner, Ranulf 1935–
    The story of yachting.
    I. Yachting to 1985
    1. Title 2. Thompson, Tim 1951—
797.1′ 24′09

Line illustrations by Ethan Danielson
Portraits by Jackie Colquhoun
Book designed by Michael Head

© Text: Ranulf Rayner 1988
© Paintings: Tim Thompson 1988

First American Edition, 1988.
All Rights Reserved.

ISBN 0-393-02652-3

W. W. Norton & Company, Inc.,
500 Fifth Avenue, New York, NY 10110.
W. W. Norton & Company, Ltd.,
37 Great Russell Street, London WC1B 3NU.

Printed in Italy

Cowes Castle, 1801. In 1858 it became home to the Royal Yacht Squadron

CONTENTS

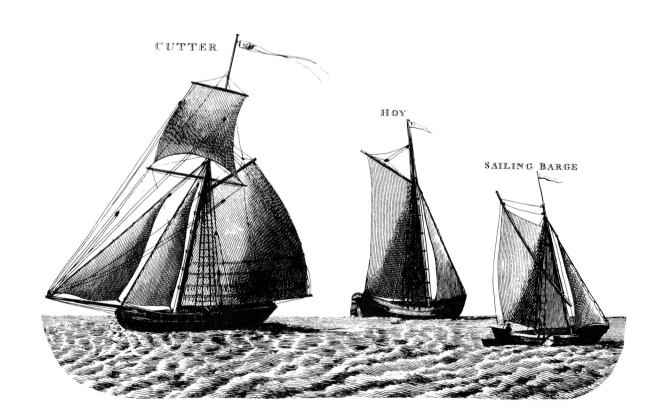

FOREWORD

Ever since I first went to sea, and this was with my father in his lovely 12 metre yacht *Copeja* some fifty-five years ago, I have been astonished by the difference between the reality of life afloat and the great moments captured by writers and artists down the centuries. Sailors have a happy way of forgetting the physical discomforts and stressful mental apprehension, and it is particularly true of sailing that 'beauty lies in the eye of the beholder'.

It is a great honour to be invited by Ranulf Rayner to write a foreword to his latest book *The Story of Yachting*, especially since the book emphasises the important role the Dutch have played in the early days of yacht building, yachting and of course their drawings and paintings of these events.

The van de Veldes, father and son, famous Dutch maritime artists of the seventeenth century, especially remembered for the atmosphere and drama of their paintings and sketches, strongly influenced Tim Thompson, the highly talented young British marine artist of today. It is with this artistic mastery that he so cleverly brings to us the earlier techniques in a modern context, and his painting of my yacht *Flyer II* surfing down the immense waves of the Roaring Forties during the 1981–2 Whitbread Round the World Race, is a particularly fine example of his art.

I have been fortunate to be able to participate in two yacht races around the world with *Flyer I* and *Flyer II*, and I believe all those who read this book will share with me the romance of sailing on a grand scale, which has been so professionally portrayed by both artist and writer.

CORNELIS VAN RIETSCHOTEN
WINNER WHITBREAD ROUND THE WORLD RACE 1977–8 AND 1981–2

Left Yachts, 1794: the Dutch influence continues

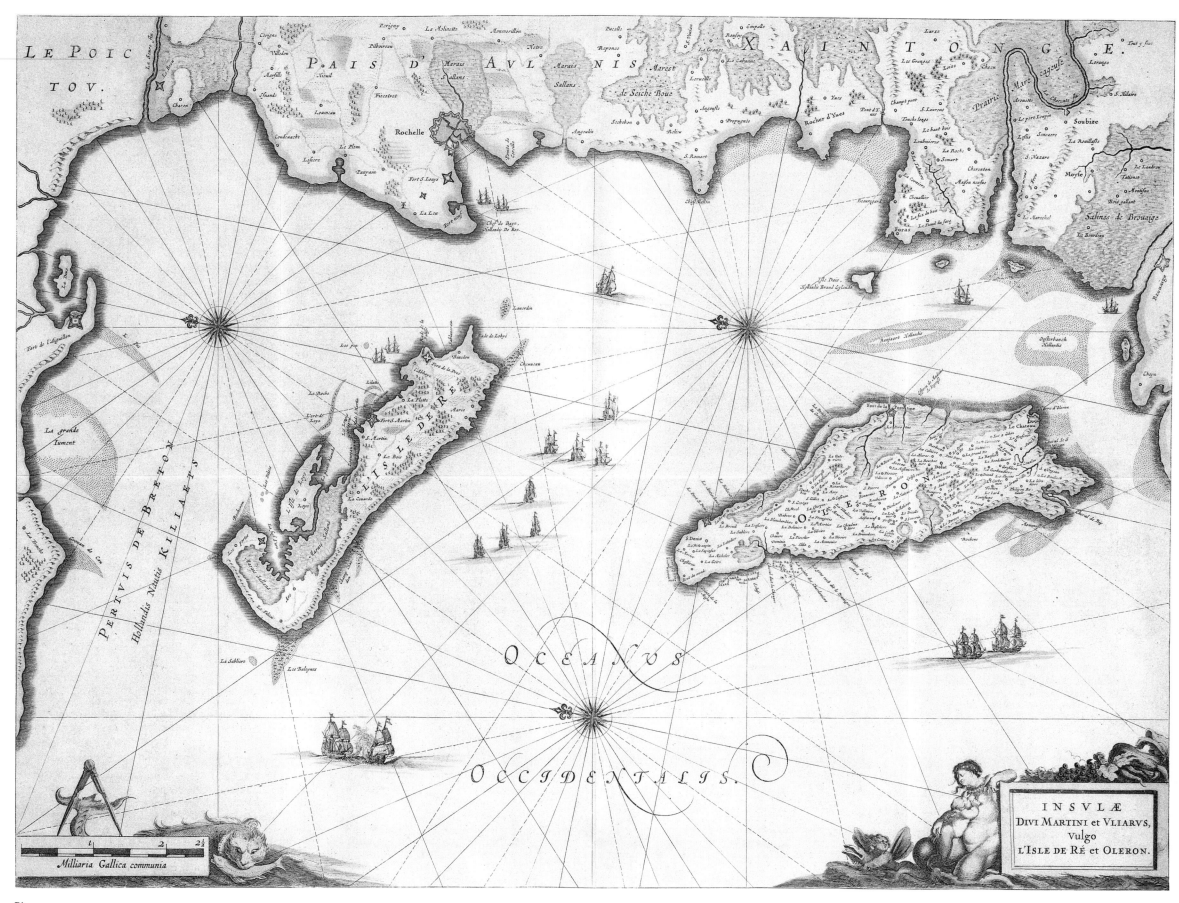

Pirate water

INTRODUCTION

Looking out of my studio window I can see the yachts bobbing on the water at Starcross almost four miles away and some nine hundred feet below. I doubt that the scene was much different when England's first yacht club was formed there over two centuries ago.

Yachts have always fascinated me and I suppose that there is nothing lovelier fashioned by man. Since the beginning of the seventeenth century they have been the subject of many beautiful paintings but their stories have often never been told.

On returning from Fremantle and the euphoria of the 1987 America's Cup, I received a surprise invitation to tell some of the forgotten stories about past contestants after dinner at the New York Yacht Club. It was an honour indeed, for no person in that illustrious building, I believed, was less qualified to lecture on the subject than myself.

'Gentlemen,' I began nervously, bolstered by wild New England duck and best Californian wine, 'while previously digging about in your splendid library, I found a story which made my hair stand on end, not about the America's Cup but surprisingly about my family. I had always believed that my Mother's forebears had started in business as emigré Huguenot silversmiths, but nothing, I discovered, could have been further from the truth. Gentlemen,' I said, 'we may well have something in common, for my family first joined the silver trade – as a bunch of bloody pirates!'

I had been warned by friends in New York not to pursue this line, but it was true. Since the yacht *America* had first pirated the silver in 1851, the challengers for the America's Cup, bound by the 'Deed of Gift' (the American set of rules), although encouraged to retrieve it, had often sailed against overwhelming odds.

The notorious family Courtaux, now Courtauld, on the other hand, were amongst those most responsible, until the close of the seventeenth century, for preventing the sport of yachting from developing at all! Operating from the Ile d'Oleron south of La Rochelle, they had threatened not only the entire French coastline, but far beyond, pirating every vessel that carried as much as a silver spoon, the odd pretty maiden or simply a keg of brandy.

My story of yachting in no way redresses the balance, but rather starts after most of the pirates had hung up their cutlasses and is about the other side of the coin. It is a tale of romance and many acts of daring, but above all it is the story about other 'gentlemen of fortune', hell bent with their great yachts in mastering the unyielding ocean, and in seeking better reward for their endeavours – from the silver of the sea.

Tim Thompson also has a studio placed high above the water from where he can see every type of vessel entering Plymouth Sound, the warships loading missiles, and the yachts sometimes going aground. Surrounded by a library of nautical books, many lying open on the floor, he works in a dust-free atmosphere where only the faint whiff of varnish gives any sense of nostalgia or feeling for those days of yore. He paints quickly with a brush which he changes constantly from a bunch in his left hand, applying layer upon layer of translucent washes until the canvas starts to glow and you feel that you are actually becoming part of the story he is so cleverly creating.

Tim studied the technique when he was a boy living on the tiny island of Herm in the Channel Islands, where he grew up in an old farmhouse with the sea lapping at the door. It started as no more than a hobby, but when he was later given a book on marine paintings for his birthday, he became so intrigued by the work of seventeenth-century Dutch marine artists that he travelled to London where he spent many hours studying the superb Van de Veldes hanging in the Maritime Museum and on other important walls.

But probably it was the lure of the treacherous rocks off the west coast of Guernsey that finally encouraged him to paint seriously, for, intrigued by the local hero Captain Saumarez and the part he had played in the Napoleonic wars, he would trace the passages the captain had reconnoitred and recreate some hair-raising battle scenes of old. It was only recently that Tim turned his attention to yachts, and for me these paintings convey much of the magic of the past.

English Royal Yachts at Sea (Willem van de Velde the Younger,
1633–1707)

EARLY YEARS

'Give quarter', cried the pirate chief, 'give quarter unto me.' – But no quarter did we give him and we sank him in the sea.

ANON

The law in the early years of yachting stretched no further than the low-water mark, and fighting afloat, until piracy was finally eliminated, was all part of the day's work if you had good enough reason to put out to sea.

The word yacht first appeared in the *Histoire de la Marine Française* as early as 1551, although no separate history of yachting appears to have been written before 1720. There is no doubt that sailing for pleasure was undertaken long before any vessel was specially constructed for the purpose, just as until the end of the eighteenth century most yachts, for reasons of safety, carried cannon for everyone to see. Today it would be hard to imagine a Nicholson or a Jongert carrying cannon, but it was certainly one early definition of a yacht. Falconer's *Marine Dictionary* of 1771 describes a yacht as 'a vessel of state, normally employed to convey princes, ambassadors or other great personages from one kingdom to another', but Burgess's *Dictionary of Sailing* is perhaps more appropriate for modern times, there not being so many sailor princes or seaside kingdoms around. 'A yacht is a private pleasure vessel or boat,' it states, 'built specifically for racing or cruising, and with living accommodation for her crew.' For the purposes of this book Burgess is close to the mark, only that the stories that follow are of both power and sailing yachts, measuring generally more than 50ft (15m).

But although the literal meaning of the word 'yacht' has never been obvious its origins, as widely accepted, stemmed most likely from the Dutch word *jagt*, probably derived from the expression *jaghen* meaning to hunt or to pursue. *Jaght schips*, described by a Dutchman in 1599 as 'swift vessels of war', were later used for Government business, for carrying merchandise or simply as a source of pleasure for all who sailed in them.

When in 1601 John Keymor had written 'There is more wealth raised out of herrings and other fish in Her Majesty's seas by neighbouring nations in one year than the King of Spain hath from the Indies in four', he was referring to the Dutch, for at that time they were probably the most successful maritime nation of them all. Blessed with vast tracts of inland waterways, it was only natural that yachting should develop not only as a national pastime but also as a business, and listed in the *Dictionnaire de Marine*, published in Amsterdam in 1702, are many yachts, probably built for official duties, measuring over 100ft (30m) and 100 tons or more. Although no records exist of these yachts subsequently being used for racing, when the skates had been put away after the winter they must have given their owners many hours of enjoyment, and it is fortunate for us that several of these fine ships are illustrated in works by the van de Veldes, Verschuring Jan Griffiere, Storck and other famous contemporary Dutch marine artists of the time.

The first occasion on which there is mention of a yacht in English literature, however, is an entry made in Evelyn's diary on 1 October 1661: 'I sail'd this morning with his Majesty in one of his yachts (or pleasure vessells) not known among us til the Dutch E. India Company presented that curious piece to the King.' Without question, therefore, the first yachts came to Great Britain from Holland at the time of the Restoration, and it was while the young Prince Charles, who had, as Samuel Pepys put it: 'a transcendent mastery of all maritime knowledge', was in exile there, that the 'curious piece' was presented to him by the Dutch on the occasion of his accession to the throne of England.

The King lost no time in promoting the new sport, and Pepys, later to be Secretary to the Admiralty, was not slow to complain of his extravagances, each yacht becoming more costly than the last. Apart from the initial payment on the many yachts that Charles II ordered, the running costs were also not inconsiderable, but Pepys, like the rest, soon found enough time to indulge in the game himself. 'We went down four or five miles (below Woolwich) with extraordinary pleasure, it being a fine day and a brave gale of wind, and had some oysters brought us aboard newly taken, which were excellent, and ate with great pleasure.' Sadly, however, the sport was not taken up by the nation and was more an expensive hobby for the Court, paid for from the Privy Purse, but with the excuse of passing on yachts, with which the King got bored quickly, to the Navy.

Just before Charles II died in 1685, his final yacht, believed to have been built once more in Holland, was again christened *Mary*. The *Princess Mary*, an 80ft (24m) two decker, was to have a remarkable history, soon afterwards being part of the escort that brought William of Orange back to England in 1689. She remained in service as a yacht until 1750, and when she was sold, history relates, and renamed the *Betsy Cairns* she became in turn an East Indiaman, a privateer, and in the reign of George III, a Government troopship, finishing her days as a collier trading out of Newcastle.

The *Princess Mary* was finally lost off the mouth of the Tyne in 1827. No wonder that during her life span of an astonishing 142 years some wit had time to record:

> Behold the fate of sublunary things:
> She exports coal, but once imported kings.

The 'yachting boom', which lasted only ten glorious years between 1660 and 1670, collapsed almost as soon as it had started. Part of the problem had been the outbreak of the Dutch war of 1665, but this was followed shortly afterwards by the Plague and the Great Fire of London, which must have had a somewhat dampening effect on the enthusiasm of both the King and his Court alike.

In 1675, only fifteen years after the arrival of the first *Mary*, from the autobiography of the Hon Roger North, it is possible to deduce that a few brave fellows were beginning to venture further afield in their sturdy yachts, and the noble sport of cruising had begun. He wrote:

> Her ordinary sail was a boom mainsail, stay forsail and a jib. . . . There was little of interest in the day's voyage, the gale brisk, the air clear, no inconvenience to molest us, nor wants to trouble our thoughts, neither business to importune, nor formalities to tease us, . . . just that the working of the vessel, its rigging, and the position of the canvas, do exercise as much of mechanics as all the other arts there are in the world.

Probably no one, even in these days of hydraulically operated rigs and stowaway sails, could have put it any better.

North (an early promoter of North Sails?) was, however, well ahead of his times, for fifty years later a similarly inclined yachtsman, Robert Wyeth, was deploring 'the want of taste in our enjoyments which we show by totally neglecting the pursuit of what seems to me the highest degree of amusement.'

A Dutch galliot with a view of Amsterdam
This drawing, and those on the following three pages, are all by
Dominic Serres, RA, and were published in 1805

THE YACHT CLUBS

Perhaps one of the highlights in the yachting scene during the early period was the visit to England by Peter the Great of Russia in 1698. A confirmed enthusiast, he worked for three months as a shipwright at Deptford, spending as much time as he could sailing on the river. With Queen Anne on the throne, such small flames soon flickered, but fortunately before they died the Queen herself preceded them, and for yachting a new and more enlightened era began.

Not surprisingly it was left to the sport-loving Irish to put yachting back on its planks again, and in 1720 there were enough nautically minded gentlemen with deep enough pockets in the county of Cork to inaugurate, under the auspices of the Hon James O'Bryen and Lord Inchiquin, the first-known yacht club. Perhaps yachting was at last getting through to the people.

From the records of the 'Water Club of Cork Harbour' it appears that the twenty-five members, however, were far more concerned with playing war

games than taking the sport seriously, and an extract from their Sailing Orders states: 'The fleet to rendezvous at Spithead, . . . any boat not being in sight by the time the Admiral is abreast of the Castle, shall forfeit one English crown towards buying gun-powder for the use of the fleet.' Their club house, which sat on the Island of Haulbowline, was scrupulously guarded by one known as the 'Knight', who, together with the Admiral, was a stickler for the rules.

Peter the Great of Russia is also claimed to have inaugurated the first yacht club, when in 1718 he lent over a hundred yachts to the people, which became known as 'the flotilla of the Neva'. But as the crews

A cutter with a view of South Sea Castle

were most likely dragooned, and not necessarily there for pleasure, the matter remains in dispute.

To follow the development of yachting we must return again to the Thames, for by the middle of the eighteenth century the sport was again becoming popular and in 1749 the eleven-year-old Prince George, later to be crowned George III, presented a silver cup to the winner of a sailing match from Greenwich to the Nore, which was the beginning of cup racing as we know it today.

In 1770 the first British yacht club was founded at Starcross in Devon, but the year 1775 is better remembered, for it marked the formation of the Cumberland

Fleet. The Duke of Cumberland, brother of George III, had given a trophy to be raced for 'from Westminster Bridge to Putney Bridge and back by pleasure-sailing boats from 2 to 5 tons burthen, and constantly lying above London Bridge.' For almost fifty seasons, the Cumberland Society, composed largely of city merchants, continued to develop the sport of yacht racing, and as it increased in popularity, matches became more numerous and were held further below the bridge.

The sea was already becoming a safer place, and the Solent, that sheltered stretch of water between England and the Isle of Wight, a mecca for yachtsmen of a much

more serious nature. One or two yachts had been bought by amateurs, followers of the Cumberland Fleet, but by 1800 the professionals were taking over and occasional contests sailed off Cowes for 'heavy wagers'.

Only one man was missing when in 1815 the Cowes yachtsmen met at the Thatched House Tavern in London to start their own club, for two weeks later the Marquis of Anglesey, owner of the famous British yacht *Pearl*, was to lose a leg at the battle of Waterloo. In 1817 the Prince Regent launched the *Royal George*,

A sloop, with Calshot Castle behind

entertaining on her lavishly, and in the same year he joined the Yacht Club, which in 1833 was given the title 'The Royal Yacht Squadron' by His Majesty.

The Thames Yacht Club came about in quite a different way. At a dinner held in London by the Cumberland Fleet in August 1823, they had decided to change their name to the Coronation Sailing Society, but because of a heated dispute over the result of a race the captains decided to break away and form a new club. The word was spreading, and in 1824 the Royal Northern Yacht Club, at Rothesay on the Firth of Clyde, was also founded, famous for its red burgees.

The story of yachting had not only spread north but far to the south as well, and in 1829 a new flag was raised on the Rock of Gibraltar. Subsequently called the Royal Gibraltar Yacht Club it was heralded as the first in the Commonwealth, and only the seventh in the world.

The following year the sport was first acknowledged in the Baltic, King Carl Johan giving his approval to the Royal Swedish Yacht Club, founded in Stockholm with headquarters at Sandhamn, the oldest foreign club listed in Lloyd's Register. Soon afterwards in 1831 the Irish Yacht Club was formed.

Then in 1837 the French held their first regatta at Dieppe, the start of a great tradition which has led to her becoming one of the most respected yachting nations, particularly in long-distance racing, of them all. Their first yacht club, established in 1840, was the Société des Régates du Havre, also known for introducing the first handicap by tonnage rule.

In 1838 the Royal Hobart Regatta Association came into being, putting the far off land of Tasmania firmly on the charts, the Sydney–Hobart race later becoming one of the leading events on the ocean. But the Royal Bermuda Yacht Club, inaugurated later in 1844, claimed to have held the first international race in

A schooner, with a view of New York

1849, and in 1906, together with the Brooklyn Yacht Club, the first ocean race from the United States to Bermuda, which is now also famous.

Surprisingly, the Dutch, having sown the seed, had been one of the slowest to get the sport of yachting growing. The Koninklijke Nederlandsche Jachtclub, founded in Rotterdam in 1846, however, was quickly followed by other Dutch clubs, and in Germany the first yacht club was established in 1855 at Königsberg.

American yachting had meanwhile long been under full sail. After the occupation of New York by the British in 1664, most of the Dutch settlers continued to live there, exerting considerable influence on the social customs of the time. There is little doubt that they also built their own yachts, although on this our history fails. Towards the stern of this book there is mention of the first of the world's great schooners being built at Gloucester in America in the year 1713, but well before that date it is known that a number of American sloop-rigged vessels had been commissioned. By 1771 there were some 125 sloops plying the Hudson River between New York and Albany. It is also recorded that in 1783 a yacht from Boston, loaded with ginseng root, made it all the way to China. But the first yacht built by Americans solely for pleasure was that from the town of Salem, Massachusetts, in 1816, costing Captain Crowninshield a cool $50,000, and christened *Cleopatra's Barge*.

On 30 July 1844, a number of gentlemen assembled on board the little 25 ton schooner *Gimcrack* lying off Manhattan, and the New York Yacht Club was founded. Although the Southern Yacht Club, formed next, might claim to be the oldest with waterfront premises, this was the earliest yacht club in the USA, and since then its first commodore, and sponsor of the yacht *America*, John Cox Stevens, has been hailed as the 'father of American Yachting'.

THE *MARY* AND KING CHARLES II

On 8 May 1660, Prince Charles was still in exile at Breda in Holland when he heard that he had been proclaimed King of England, and no sooner had the Dutch Government been made aware of this information than they put a number of vessels at his command. Adrian Vlackett, writing in 1660 said:

> The yacht on board the King sailed had been built for himself by the Prince of Orange, but now belongs to the Board of Admiralty of Rotterdam, and it was without doubt the finest of the little fleet, which consisted, without other ships, almost countless, of thirteen large yachts, which the persons of rank use in the rivers and on the sea, to pass from one province to another, for necessity as well as for pleasure.

Later that month, arriving at Delft, the King was rowed from Scheveningen to join the warship *Naseby*, which, renamed in deference the *Royal Charles*, then carried him home across the Channel. Vlackett continues: . . . 'The King had found his yacht so convenient and comfortable, that he remarked, while discoursing with the deputies, that he might order one of the same style, so soon as she would arrive in England.' Mindful of his fatherland, the burgermaster of Amsterdam, knowing of a yacht of similar size but

Charles II

HMY *Mary* arriving with Princess Mary at Gravesend, 12 February 1689 (Willem van de Velde the Younger, 1633–1707)

not yet fitted out, offered her to the King, who 'did not absolutely accept it, but at the same time did not refuse.' And so the Board of Admiralty at Rotterdam 'had the interior of the cabins decorated and gilded, while some of the best artists have been engaged in making beautiful paintings and sculptures with which to embellish it within and without'.

The *Mary*, as the King named her, was 66ft (20m) in overall length, 19ft (5.8m) in the beam, 10ft (3m) in draught and of 100 tons burden. She carried eight guns and a complement of between twenty and thirty men. Rigged with a sprit mainsail and staysail, she was equipped with the customary Dutch leeboards and her circular gun ports were surrounded by wreaths of gold. The King was delighted and in truth could not wait to take delivery, on 15 August 1660, Samuel Pepys entering in his diary: 'To the office, and after dinner to White Hall, where I found the King gone this morning by 5 of the clock to see a Dutch pleasure-boat below the bridge.' This is the only known authentic account of the arrival of the *Mary* in England, and later Pepys leaves us in no doubt that the King was most thrilled with her and was soon sailing her extensively, sometimes taking her helm and with an escort of warships visiting places along the Kentish coast.

During his reign some twenty-eight yachts were launched from the royal dockyards for the King and his brother, later to become James II, including a second yacht *Mary*, built to the original boat's plans. Most of these vessels were designed by Phineas and Christopher Pett, who were descended from a family famous for building ships from the time of Henry VIII, and various attempts were made to improve their stability and speed, but without any dramatic effect. Some interesting costs of building the Duke of York's *Anne*, an eight gunner, almost identical to the Dutch *Mary*, were:

	£	s	d		£	s	d
Hull	1,815	2	4	Gilding ...	160	0	0
Rig	240	12	0	Carving ..	144	10	0
Lead	324	0	0	Ironworks	52	18	1
Guns ...	186	9	10	Brassiers .	16	0	0
Colours	124	5	5	Platerers .	28	13	4

And for a mariner's pay – just 1½ pence per day.

It was the *Anne* and another new yacht, the King's *Katherine*, named after the lady he was to marry in the following year, which in 1661 were the first yachts known to have been involved in a race, with the *Merry Monarch*, as he came to be called, winning the then handsome wager of £100.

But as new yachts were built the *Mary* soon drifted into disfavour, and having been sent to the Irish station, her crew begged the Navy Commissioners, 'that their families may not be starved in the streets, and themselves go like heathen, having nothing to cover their nakedness, being owed 52 weeks pay.' To seamen in the seventeenth century Navy it was often the case, but for the *Mary* it was the beginning of the end. Sadly she rotted away with neglect, sinking off Holyhead in 1675, where she was found by divers in 1973, fortunately being left to rest in the peaceful grave she most certainly deserved.

Only one unfinished and foreshortened drawing, by the Dutch artist Jan Beerstraten, of a yacht bearing the Royal Arms of England, probably the *Mary*, is known to exist. This painting by Tim Thompson of Charles II revisiting Dover in 1661, soon after her arrival in England, has been reconstructed from the drawing and a rare manuscript of the period

Mary

NINETEENTH-CENTURY YACHTING

WATERWITCH AND THE ROYAL NAVY

Yacht matches had been held in England since 1775, but it was not until the beginning of the nineteenth century, when Cowes on the Isle of Wight became fashionable to yachtsmen, that the sport there really came alive.

In about the year 1800 a Mr Weld from Dorset had built himself a cutter *Lulworth Castle*, and his enthusiasm for the sport won him many wagers. His son Joseph inherited his father's passion for racing and in 1826 won the first race staged by the Yacht Club at Cowes. But although it was also the first race ever to be run for a cup, it was not the end of the wagers, and the tremendous rivalry that followed between members of the club was largely responsible for the birth of yacht racing as we know it today.

The Royal Navy had also become interested in smaller fore and aft rigged vessels and in the year 1800 owned no less than forty schooners, surprisingly most of foreign build. Apart from those either captured from the French or taken from the Spanish, many of these vessels had been built in America, where the sport of yachting was also gathering momentum. There, in 1811, the brothers Swain of New Jersey were to patent the 'lee board through the bottom' or centreboard, and later, in 1835, the Americans were also to hold their first yacht race. The naval schooners had been acquired to compete with the British Revenue cutters which in turn had been built to outsail the smuggling ships at that time. Charles Ratsey of the famous sailmaking family recounted: 'The port of Cowes was then conspicuous for building large cutters both for the Excise and the smugglers side by side, the smuggling business being extensively carried out from this port at the beginning of the nineteenth century.' But it really needed yachtsmen to get the situation finally under control.

It was some years after the establishment of the Yacht Club before the annual regatta became a feature of Cowes. In those early years it was quite customary for yachts to carry an armoury of cutlasses which no doubt gave their owners a considerable feeling of security. Sometimes, however, they were put to other uses.

In 1829 Joseph Weld and his yacht *Lulworth* had become involved in a bitter duel with another leading yachtsman, Lord Belfast, and his yacht *Louisa*. They had been racing down the Solent neck and neck, but as they were about to cross the finishing line off Cowes, *Lulworth*, on the port tack, collided with *Louisa* which was on the starboard tack. It was already dark and as fireworks lit up the night sky *Louisa*'s crew drew their cutlasses and set about hacking down the *Lulworth*'s rigging, leaving her disabled. It was quite literally a fight to the finish.

Following the launching of Weld's famous cutter *Alarm* in 1830, the duel continued, each claiming that his own yacht was faster. But although Belfast challenged *Alarm*'s owner to countless matches throughout the season, Weld steadfastly refused to race him, meanwhile winning all the club trophies. Belfast was furious, but a year later he had his revenge. In September 1831, recognising that the *Alarm* was the better boat on smooth water, Lord Belfast challenged Joseph Weld to a match 'round the Owers' for a thousand pounds, which he surprisingly accepted. Stations were tossed for on *Louisa*'s deck, and at six in the morning they started from Spithead. *Louisa* gradually pulled away finishing alone in light airs at four the following morning off Cowes Castle. 'I have proved to the world that I possess the fastest cutter afloat,' crowed Lord Belfast, 'and I will now see what I can do with a square-rigger.' (Some said that the Yacht Club at Cowes was later conferred with the title 'Royal' owing to Lord Belfast's successes.)

Many yachts in the 1880s were fine sea-going vessels, built, manned and rigged in imitation of brigs in the Royal Navy, and indeed it was not unusual for them to be commanded by naval officers on shore leave. Brass work was kept burnished at all times and general shipshapeness was regarded with much greater importance than speed. However, *Waterwitch* was different. Launched from East Cowes by Lady Belfast in 1832, *Waterwitch* was fitted out with cannon, weights and shot like a man-of-war. At that time there was a famous naval gun brig that used to sail through Cowes Roads 'with a good deal of boasting', and, determined to cut her down to size, *Waterwitch* was sent at once to search her out. Eventually she fell on her off the coast of Portugal and having defeated her on all points of sailing she returned to Cowes in triumph.

It was only the beginning of a glorious game of cat and mouse. Lying up in the lee of a headland and within reach of a good tavern, *Waterwitch* would often wait for a suitable naval ship to leave Portsmouth harbour. Then Lord Belfast, who had become a bit of an old pirate, would suddenly command his crew to make sail. Drill on the *Waterwitch* was immaculate, and she was so quick at overhauling the opposition that Belfast would then shorten sail to rub salt in the wound. Two years later, *Waterwitch* challenged any square-rigger afloat to a race around the Eddystone Rocks, and after a remarkable win, she was sold to serve her country with distinction in the fleet and to subsequently influence the ship design of the entire British Navy.

AN ACCOUNT OF THE TIMES

The following account by Charles Ratsey gives us an idea of the similarity of both friend and foe in the 1830s:

A celebrated smuggler was named *John Susannah*, with fourteen guns, well known to my father as being a very smart and efficient cutter, and well manned in every respect. This vessel, having committed some depredation, was reported by the Government to be 'outlawed', and HM gun brig *Osprey* was dispatched to capture her. The two vessels met off Christchurch Head, and the smuggler cleared for action. In the first broadside Capt. Allen of the *Osprey* was killed, but, after a desperate struggle the smuggler was taken and brought to Cowes. There was but one man hung, named Coombs, having been picked out for firing after the colours were struck. He was hung upon a gibbet at Stony Point, the body hanging for many months.

'Paint me the old *America*,' I'd say, 'or the death of the *Valkyrie*,
Or the *Waterwitch* as I sailed in once in my young days at sea,
Shipshape and Bristol fashion, too, as a great yacht ought to be . . .

'An' you might do 'er outward bound, with a sky full o' clouds,
An' the dinghy just droppin' astern, an' gulls flyin' in crowds,
An' the decks shiny-wet with rain, and the wind shakin' the shrouds . . .'

Waterwitch

THE YACHTS OF JOSEPH WELD

The book, *Memorials of the Royal Yacht Squadron*, published in 1903, states: 'There has probably never been a great sport so dominated by the personality of one man as was yachting from its infancy by Mr Joseph Weld.'

Thomas Weld, Joseph's father, had decided to build his first yacht in 1784, but in those days there was no such thing as a yacht builder and the Lulworth Estate carpenters found it a little beyond them working on the beach at Arish Mell in Dorset. Eventually, when it became obvious that her designer also had little idea how to launch her, 'leaving her stranded like a fish of the porpoise kind', as Thomas remarked, he had to hire himself a shipwright named Williams, who later built him other boats including one called the *Castle*, which, when he died, was left to Joseph. In 1815 Joseph, with his new yacht *Charlotte*, had already become a devoted yachtsman. He had always greatly admired the fast cutters involved in the smuggling trade, and in 1821 he had the *Arrow*, a cutter of 84 tons, built at Lymington with the intention of racing her.

The early sailing matches were boisterous affairs, and although normally raced for a purse of gold, they were often held in an atmosphere of extreme provocation. In 1826 *The Sporting Magazine* reporting on the first Town Cup held at Cowes commented: 'When only a few miles from home the *Arrow* had the temer-ity to cross the *Miranda* and the two vessels became entangled. The gallant Sir James Jordan had a narrow escape from a dreadful blow aimed at the back of his head by one of Mr Weld's men with a handspike. He avoided the blow and floored the rascal with tremendous violence.' But *Arrow* went on to win comfortably. It was the start of *Arrow*'s astonishingly successful career, and the following year she won a trophy presented by King George IV. Meanwhile he also commissioned the great yacht *Lulworth*, and in 1830 the even better known bluff-bowed cutter *Alarm*.

In 1851 both the *Arrow*, now under the ownership of Mr Thomas Chamberlayne, and the *Alarm*, were amongst the fourteen yachts contesting the Hundred Guineas Cup with the yacht *America*. At the Nab light vessel, marking the eastern end of the course, *Arrow* was in the lead when *America*, it was said, following a second set of rules, cut inside, and although chased by the rest of the fleet, put herself into such a commanding position, that the *Arrow*, attempting to pass her again off Ventnor, ran aground. The *Alarm* turned to rescue her, but in doing so was also left behind and retired.

Both cutters were altered to the lines of *America* very soon afterwards and continued their distinguished careers by winning many races. Joseph Weld, who died in 1863, was allowed to sail on the *Alarm*, a privilege denied his Catholic family, only because he refused to interfere with the crew's flowery language.

The *Arrow*, 1826

America

20

Aurora   Freak   Alarm   Arrow   Volante

Memorials wrote: 'One only has to think of the relative merits of
the *Alarm* and the *Aurora*, which ran the *America* so closely, to
be convinced of the luck of *America* in finding Mr Weld's great
cutter so early out of the race.'

THE *AMERICA'S* REVOLUTION

As the shadows lengthened on the afternoon of 23 August 1851, the day of the Hundred Guineas Cup, Queen Victoria, summoned to the deck of her yacht the *Victoria and Albert*, waiting for the leaders to appear south-west of the Isle of Wight, watched spellbound as the rakish black hull of the schooner *America* rounded St Catherine's Point and came charging down towards the Needles, out on her own. When she passed the Royal Yacht, Commodore Stevens first saluted and then gave three cheers with his crew, and the Queen, accompanied by Prince Albert and the nine-year-old Prince Edward of Wales, waved in cheerful acknowledgement. 'Where is the second?', she asked her captain. 'There is no second, Your Majesty', he replied.

Many a yacht has had a better racing record than the *America*, indeed from her fifty races that followed, she won only twelve. But probably no other boat in history has had such a profound effect on the future of yacht design. 'She has a low, black hull, two noble sticks of extreme rake without an extra rope, and is altogether the beau-ideal of what one is accustomed to read about in Cooper's novels,' *Bell's Life* had quoted a few days earlier.

'Yacht building is an art in which England is unrivalled', crowed another publication, *Yacht List*, 'and she is distinguished pre-eminently and alone for the perfection of science in handling them.' While the

The Marquis of Anglesey, a respected member of the Royal Yacht Squadron and owner of the yacht *Pearl*

Waterloo veteran, the Marquis of Anglesey, remarked crustily: 'If she is right, then all of us are wrong.'

The challenge from America, promoted by some New York businessmen and managed by John C. Stevens, the first commodore of the New York Yacht Club, was quickly hitting the headlines. 'A large proportion of the peerage and gentry of the United Kingdom forsook the sports of the moors', stated *The Times* (the grouse shooting season having begun), 'to witness the struggle between the yachtsmen of England, hitherto unmatched and unchallenged, and the Yankees who had crossed the Atlantic to meet them.'

For the British the result of the race was nothing less than a disaster and although there was a second yacht home, the gallant *Aurora*, which had crept up after the Needles, finishing just eighteen minutes behind, it was a lesson that the home team could not afford to ignore. 'I've learned one thing,' exclaimed the Marquis of Anglesey later, and after much deliberation, 'I've been sailing my yacht stern foremost for the last twenty years!'

In *America*, the New York pilot boats, two-masted schooners more than 80ft (24m) long, had gained a world-wide reputation for speed, and George Steers, creator of *America*, had drawn the lines of the best of them. Some of his ideas were well ahead of their time, and it is interesting that when *America* was rebuilt by Pitchers of Northfleet in 1858, Henry Liggins, head joiner, noted later: 'I can remember well, as if it were but yesterday, sitting on her new English oak timbers and picking up the snuff-like rubbish of her original construction.' It is likely, therefore, that not only were her lines radical in British terms, but also that she had been built of unusually light material. The secret of *America*'s success, however, was not at once appreciated by British yacht builders, and although a number of existing yachts were altered to conform immediately, it took some time to sink in. The famous designer G. L. Watson, years afterwards, wrote: 'The run, though rather short, was very fair, the buttock lines, especially, showing beautifully easy curves. Her flat sails of machine spun cotton, laced to her booms, gaffs and masts . . . only enhanced her form.' She was a winner it was true, but her success was long attributed to the material of her sails.

The remainder of *America*'s history is a surprising and romantic story, too long to write in any detail. While British designers were still scratching their heads, *America* was sold to Lord John De Blaquière, and for the next ten years remained, for all to copy, on the British side of the Atlantic. When the Civil War broke out in America, however, she was bought by a man from Savannah, and for a time served the South as a blockade runner. Chased by a Union gunboat up the

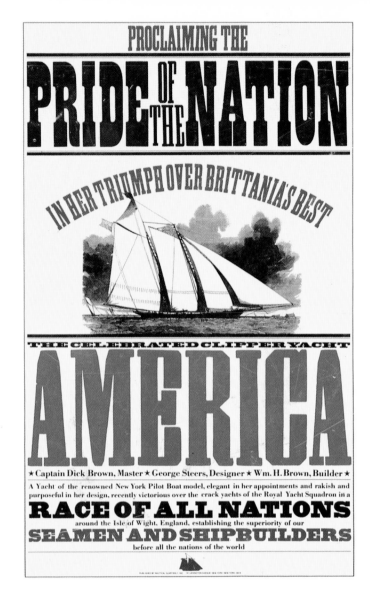

St John's River, she was unfortunately sunk but later raised, and in 1863 she was sailed north to Annapolis, becoming a training ship at the Naval Academy there. In 1870, having been restored, *America* defended her now famous title in a race won by the American schooner *Magic*, and appeared once more, *hors concours*, in the America's Cup of 1876. She had meanwhile been bought by General Butler for $5,000 at a naval auction, and in 1901, her last season in commission, she took G. L. Watson and the great Sir Thomas Lipton for a sail. In 1921 a benevolent group of yachtsmen acquired her for a dollar and returned her to the Academy as a gift to the nation, where in 1945, having attracted countless tourists, she was sadly scrapped, outliving her young designer by almost ninety years.

America salutes the Queen

Victoria & Albert   *America*

THE STEAM YACHTS

THE *MENAI* AND THE *NORTH STAR*

Rivalry between Lord Belfast and certain members of the Royal Yacht Club had become so intense by the end of the 1820s that Joseph Weld built his famous cutter *Alarm* principally 'to larn Belfast', and a Mr Assheton-Smith, once greeted by Napoleon as 'le premier Chasseur d'Angleterre' because of his love of hunting hounds, announced that 'he had determined to take his future aquatic excursions' instead 'in a steam vessel of extraordinary power.'

Such threats did not go unnoticed, and, echoing the sentiments of the *Southampton Herald*, which in 1825 had condemned the Solent packet boats for their 'murky vomitings', the members passed the following resolution:

Resolved that as a material object of the Club is to promote seamanship and the improvements of sailing vessels, to which the application of steam engines is inimical, no vessel propelled by steam shall be admitted into the Club and any member applying a steam engine to his yacht shall be disqualified thereby and cease to be a member.

North Star

And so Assheton-Smith, who had ordered England's first steam yacht, the *Menai*, resigned.

The Royal Yacht Squadron, as the club became, was not, luckily, to remain intransigent for ever, and when 'Queen Victoria,' wrote Heckstall-Smith, 'in order to keep up with the Hohenzollerns and the Romanoffs' decided that she too should have a steam yacht, they were inclined to think again, and in 1853 the resolution was scrapped.

In that same year, Cornelius Vanderbilt, who was fifty-nine years old, had launched his *North Star*, the first steam yacht in America. Vanderbilt had started his working life as a farm hand on Staten Island, and, borrowing $100 from his mother, had then bought a small boat to carry passengers around New York Bay. Soon he had built up a fleet of ships, earning himself the unofficial title of 'The Commodore', and in 1849 he had increased his fortunes by running thousands of gold seekers half-way to California.

North Star was a hefty oaken 270ft (83m) steam yacht, rigged as a brigantine, with side wheel paddles 34ft (10m) in diameter. She had been built to accommodate Vanderbilt's large family in ten luxurious state rooms, each complete with rosewood furniture and silk hangings, and with a stove to keep out the damp. Costing more than $90,000, she was a superb ship on which no expense had been spared, and with $11,000,000 in his pocket The Commodore could no doubt afford to run her, for he was already, it was believed, the richest man in the world.

On 19 May 1853 *North Star* left New York bound for Southampton with her owner, his wife, ten of their twelve children, each with their personal maids, seven sons-in-law, a physician, a chaplain and the ship's cat. They were destined to meet the Russian imperial family and to visit Norway, the Baltic, France and Italy in a journey of over 15,000 miles during which *North Star* was to consume no less than 2,200 tons of coal.

One hour before sailing, the stokers had gone on strike for more pay and the chaplain, writing later about The Commodore, who was an ill-natured tyrant at the best of times, noted: 'True to his principles of action in all his business affairs, Mr Vanderbilt refused to be coerced by the seeming necessity of the case and he would not listen for a moment to the demands so urged.' The men were fired and new stokers signed on from the jetty.

North Star had taken only four months to complete

Commodore Vanderbilt

the round trip, and this had so impressed New York yachting society that, after the American Civil War, steam yachts quickly gained in popularity, in comfort and in size. It is interesting to note that in 1870 the New York Yacht Club had only four steam yachts registered, none larger than a schooner of 275 tons, but thirty years later there were more than two hundred vessels owned by club members, the largest of them being over 2,000 tons. Many of these floating palaces were used on the New York to Newport milk run, and as speed became almost as important as luxury, slower yachts were discarded, and the 170 mile cruise to the summer playgrounds became a race to cover the distance in less than seven hours.

North Star, sadly, on returning home from her successful maiden voyage, and true to the owner's grasping character, was converted as a passenger ship and eventually sold. The Commodore meanwhile had quickly got back into the driving seat, and, turning his attention to the railroads, by 1877 had increased his net worth to a staggering $40,000,000.

North Star passes the Sandy Hook lightship on her way out into the Atlantic. Previously, on leaving New York harbour, she had backed on to a reef, but had been passed fit to continue by the US Navy

North Star   *Sandy Hook LV*

THE *CORSAIRS*

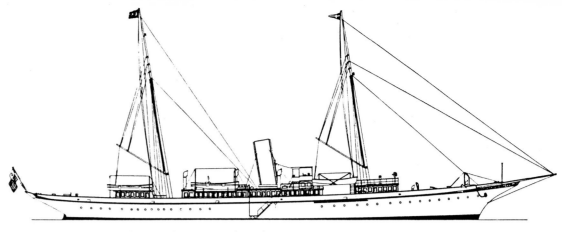

Corsair III

While Commodore Vanderbilt was away cruising on *North Star*, he had left some of his affairs in the charge of two men, Garrison and Morgan, who were expected to pay him a commission. They did not, and when The Commodore returned he sent them a brief note: 'Gentlemen, you have undertaken to cheat me. I won't sue you, for the law is too slow. I will ruin you.' And he did.

History does not relate if that Morgan had anything in common with John Pierpoint Morgan, but it is unlikely, for by the early 1900s, like Vanderbilt before him, J.P. had, through his $1,500,000,000 Steel Trust, become the most powerful tycoon of all. Morgan's famous comment about yachts, 'If you have to ask how much it costs, you can't afford it', has long been the byword of yacht brokers, but with his enduring passion for great yachts, he followed it to the letter. The number of activities he was involved in were endless, and among his philanthropic deeds were restoring churches, founding schools and national museums, providing the land for the New York Yacht Club and paying for several America's Cup defenders besides. It was hardly surprising that when he died with an estate valued at $77.5 million, John D. Rockefeller commented, 'and to think that he wasn't even a rich man.'

Morgan spent a fortune on his yachts, *Corsair I*, his first magnificent steam vessel, being acquired from a member of the New York Yacht Club in 1881 so that he could use her as a ferry between his office in New York and his home up the Hudson River. He soon found that he could conduct his business on her in greater privacy, but better still, once on board, nobody, unless they agreed his terms, could ever escape. But she was soon eclipsed by larger New York based yachts, and so in 1891 he asked the Irish expatriate K. Beavor-Webb, to design him a vessel 240ft

John Pierpoint Morgan

(73m) long. *Corsair II* was a fine looking vessel and Morgan used her constantly until 1898 when he turned her over to the Navy, asking Beavor-Webb to create an even longer yacht for him on much the same lines.

Corsair III, some would eulogise, was probably the most handsome steam yacht ever built. Beautifully proportioned, her rakish looks gave her such an air of authority that she gained countless admirers wherever she went. At 305ft (93m), she was about 60ft (18m) longer than her predecessor, and apart from being more powerful, she also had, for better manoeuvrability, a twin screw. But Morgan insisted that in every other respect, from her gilded figurehead to the pattern of the carpets, she should be exactly the same.

One particular feature of *Corsair* was her engine room. From the deckhouse it was possible to see the highly polished cylinders with all other working parts finished in bright enamel, and the whole compartment was panelled in pale maple to show up the tiniest speck of oil. Morgan was now really enjoying his yachting, and as far as he was concerned, his ship had to be as immaculate as any.

At one time Morgan was a member of no less than twenty different New York men's clubs, but not content, he started his own Corsair Club for city friends, who liked to come aboard and spend an evening with him playing cards. In 1882 he had become a member of the New York Yacht Club, and in 1899 on becoming the Club's commodore, he immediately appointed *Corsair III* as the club's flagship.

Corsair was seldom idle and often she was sent ahead of her owner to meet him on the far side of the Atlantic, possibly in Cannes, Cowes or Kiel. Her crew were renowned for their loyalty, and Captain Porter, who had been with her almost from the start, joined her again during World War I, following J.P.'s death in 1913. She had been converted to carry 134 officers and men, and, painted grey with her bowsprit removed and a wheelhouse added, was hardly recognisable. At one stage she steamed over 19,000 miles without shutting down her boilers, but she came through with flying colours and, restored to her former glory, she re-

turned to the bosom of the family until finally replaced in 1930 by *Corsair IV*.

Good ships often die hard, and it was not until 1944, after active service once again during World War II, that she was finally towed to the breakers to meet an unbefitting end. The New York Yacht Club, however, still rings with her owner's name, and a model man-of-war, presented by John Pierpoint Morgan, now stands where the America's Cup once stood, as a reminder of the days of his *Defender* and his twice-winning yacht *Columbia*, and of achievements that few, if any, can any longer attain.

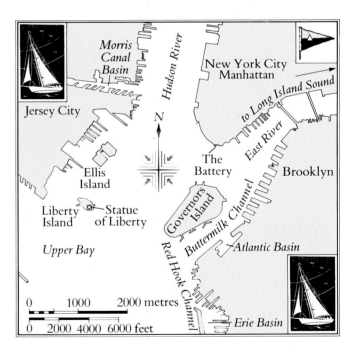

New York Harbour

Heckstall-Smith recalls in his book *All Hands on the Main Sheet*: 'After a cruise of about eight days the *Corsair* steamed back to New York, up the harbour, past the pale green Statue of Liberty, on a grey, rather smoky, afternoon. The sun, just breaking through upon it, was effective, also just tipping the pointed skyscrapers with gold.'

Corsair III

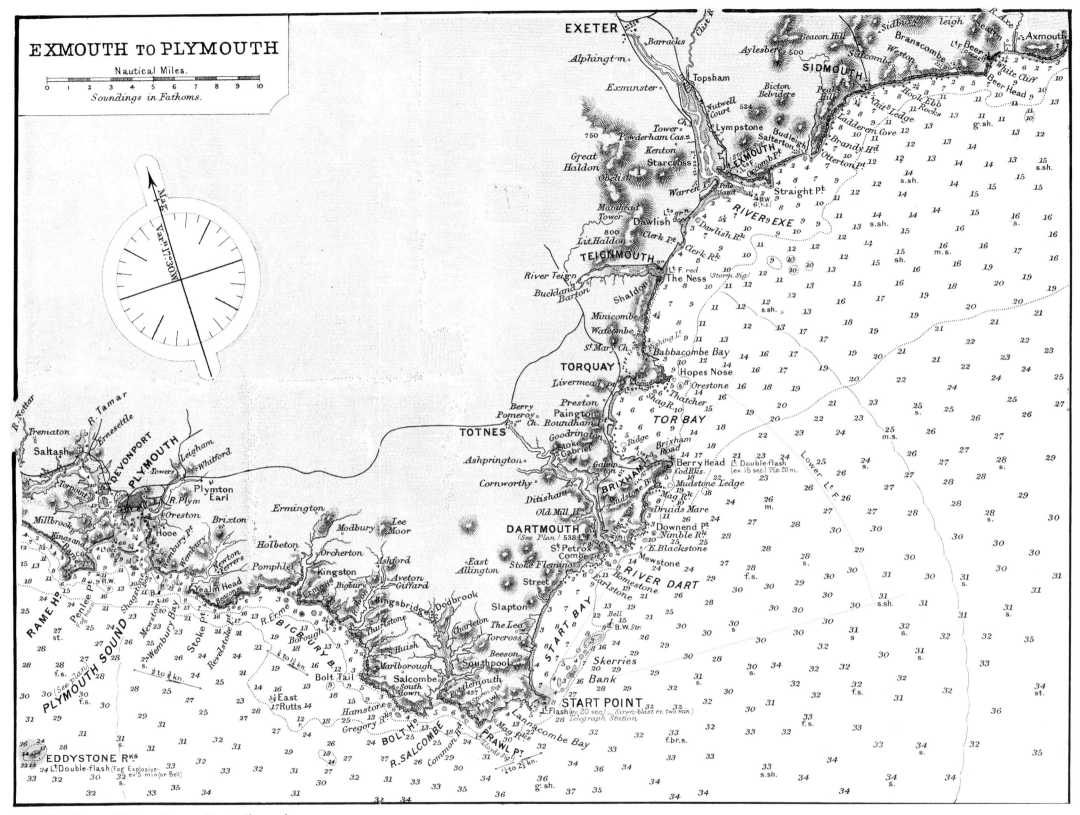

The West Country Big Boat Regatta Circuit: Plymouth,
Dartmouth and Torbay

THE
BRITANNIA ERA
1893–1936

From her launching in 1893 to her demise in 1936 the King's *Britannia* presided over perhaps the greatest years in the history of British yachting. Such magnificent racing yachts have never been seen since, and it was to the credit of the British Crown that 'Big Boating' remained fashionable for so long.

The thrill of racing these great yachts is captured in this fine action photograph taken from the deck of *Britannia* and in the words of the famous British marine author of that time, Anthony Heckstall-Smith:

It is well-nigh impossible to put into words the exhilaration one feels as one stands on the sloping deck, the wheel straining in one's hands, the great sweep of the mainsail towering above one, the blocks of the mainsheet making their own peculiar creaking noise over one's shoulder, the salt spray and spindrift flying upwards from the lee shrouds and the plunging stem that seems an infinite distance away. All the tremendous power of the hard pressed hull, the great lead keel below weighing hundreds of tons and the thousands of square feet of straining canvas aloft, is in one's hands as they grip the wheel pulling and wrenching at every muscle in one's body. And through that wheel, the trembling nerves of the great vessel vibrate to one's fingers on the spokes. The slightest variation in the wind's force is instantly communicated to one, so that the yacht becomes a living creature to be driven just so hard but not one degree harder lest, with a crack like a pistol shot, a cleat is torn from the deck or a rigging screw breaks and in a crash of splintering wood, flailing wires and rending canvas, the mast goes over the side.

Britannia, unlike most of her contemporaries, never was dismasted, and she performed so well in high winds that certain conditions came to be known by yachtsmen as 'Britannia weather'.

In her heyday she became one of the most feared yachts on the racing circuit. Starting on the Thames during May, the hotly contested big boat regattas moved to Dover and then the Solent before going north to the Clyde. From there the yachts raced off the Irish coast before returning to the Solent for Cowes Week at the end of July. After Cowes they headed west, and racing culminated with the popular Torquay, Dartmouth and Plymouth Regattas.

It was the era of power and majesty, of tremendous rivalry and feats of yachting that have seldom been surpassed. If there had been television then, audiences would have been captivated, just as the crowds of spectators at the time were captivated, by the awesome splendour of such billowing clouds of sail.

Britannia's helm
'. . . and the wheel's kick
and the wind's song
    and the white sails shaking.'

From *Salt-Water Ballads* (1902),
by John Masefield (1878–1967)

THE KING'S *BRITANNIA*

Launched in April 1893 from the Partick yard on the Clyde, and designed by the acknowledged genius G. L. Watson, *Britannia* was one of the most remarkable racing yachts of all time. In the eyes of her public no vessel has probably ever been held in greater esteem and affection – for not only was the King's yacht exceedingly beautiful, she was also brilliantly successful.

When commissioned by the Prince of Wales, later crowned Edward VII, *Britannia* initially came in for a great deal of criticism. Her long outward curving stem or 'viking bow' at first seemed out of keeping with the inward curving 'clipper bows' of the time, and her 10,000sq ft (929sq m) of canvas was generally considered far too heavy for 'the somewhat turbulent winds and waters around our coasts'. But her sail-spread and sturdy hull were to prove a winning combination and she confounded her critics in her very first season's racing.

At *Britannia*'s long white tiller as she left on her 750 mile maiden voyage to the Thames, John Carter, her first sailing master, must have soon sensed her poten-

tial, and before the month had passed she had won her spurs. The fifty-mile course was down the Lower Hope, out to the Mouse lightship, and then back up the Thames to finish off Gravesend. Crowds of spectators lined the river bank and when the big cutters, with their huge jackyard topsails in hand, came into sight with their spars glistening in the afternoon sunshine, a cheer went up as *Britannia*, with her royal racing flag flying for the first time, led the great yachts *Valkyrie II*, *Calluna* and *Iverna* over the finishing line.

It was only the beginning. Public interest in *Britannia* increased rapidly with each successful race, and her final score for her first season was an astonishing thirty-three firsts from forty-three starts and the best aggregate of the entire fleet. Her thirty crew members were delighted.

Britannia's debut had been no 'beginner's luck' and her second season was even more memorable. Early in the spring the Prince of Wales took his yacht to the Mediterranean and she won all seven races on his favourite French Riviera. On returning home she trounced the Yankee yacht *Vigilant*, which in 1893 had defeated *Valkyrie II* for the America's Cup. Indeed, by the close of her fifth season she had not only paid for her keep in prize money, but had almost reimbursed her royal owner the £10,000 she had cost him to build.

1897, however, had seen a rapid decline in the big class and partly due to new rating rules many yachts vanished from the scene. *Britannia*'s own racing flag was hauled down, and not to be seen again for fifteen years. Meanwhile she was to change hands no less than six times, twice being repurchased by royal command, firstly in order to act as a trial horse for Sir Thomas Lipton's America's Cup challenger *Shamrock I*, and secondly, after Edward VII's coronation, in 1902 as the royal cruising yacht. Two years earlier her previous owner Sir Richard Williams-Bulkeley had reduced her rig to that of a snugly built family cruiser, but the King had hankered after her and, having resigned as commodore of the Royal Yacht Squadron, for the next few seasons he and the Queen went summer sailing on *Britannia* around the coast of his beloved kingdom. She missed, therefore, much of the revival of the 'big class' starting in 1906, and having become the property of King George V in February 1911 she was not to be raced again until his new representative, the famous Major Philip Hunloke, entered her with limited success in the handicap classes of 1913.

After World War I, which then intervened, many said that *Britannia*'s racing days were numbered. But having languished in a mud-berth for several years the King refitted her and her return to the regatta circuit in July 1920 was nothing less than triumphant. Still in her

George V

old clothes, she met the fastest modern vessels of that time including *Nyria*, *White Heather* and the famous American-built schooner *Westward*. Once again the old lady showed her paces and so deep was the King's respect for her that he put her back into racing rig, completely rejuvenating her by 1922. The following season *Britannia*, now thirty years old, won twenty-three flags out of twenty-six starts, and met the first big cutter raced under Bermudian rig.

Britannia's sail was again altered in 1926 and 1927 to keep pace with the growing competition, but only in 1931 did the King agree to refit her as a Bermudian cutter. Although brilliantly handled by Philip Hunloke (later Sir Philip), she was never again to be so clever on the wind, and by 1934 she had gracefully retired to the rear of the fleet. Her last race was sailed at Cowes on 10 August 1935.

When George V died the following year, he left instructions that if none of his sons wanted the yacht, *Britannia* should be broken up. It was left to Sir Philip to arrange her funeral and at the end of June her booms and blocks, sails and cordage, were all put under the hammer. Then, just two weeks later when the tide was right, *Britannia* was launched for the last time into the Medina, a garland of flowers on her stemhead, placed there by the yard foreman. A little before midnight on 9 July two destroyers, *Amazon* and *Winchester*, came for her, and then she was towed, a forlorn hulk, out past the Needles light and St Catherine's Point to her final resting place somewhere south of the Isle of Wight.

Edward VIII had no special love of the sea, and when George V died he agreed that *Britannia* should be sunk. During his only race as king on the great yacht, he drove golf balls off her stern, as he had done years earlier much to the annoyance of his father, off the castle at Cowes on the Isle of Wight

Edward VII

Shamrock IV   *Royal Yacht Squadron*   *Britannia*

INCIDENT ON THE CLYDE 1894

On Thursday 5 July 1894, shortly before the start of the race in which His Majesty's yacht *Britannia* was competing on the Clyde for the Muir Challenge Cup, the two great yachts *Satanita* and *Valkyrie II* collided, resulting in the tragic death of one crew member and the loss of the *Valkyrie*. The disaster was to have surprising consequences.

Valkyrie II had been built for the Earl of Dunraven, to the design of George Watson, to compete for the America's Cup of 1893, in which she raced against *Vigilant*. She was an unlucky boat, for in the third and final race, when leading by almost two minutes at the final mark, her spinnaker had split and she had been overhauled by *Vigilant* just before the finish. In many ways she was a sister ship to *Britannia*, and they were competing together on that misty Scottish morning some nine months later on the Clyde.

Satanita, designed by Joseph Soper in 1892, was then the longest cutter ever built and she was to hold the speed record of over sixteen knots, timed between the Nab and Owers lightships, for a great number of years. Indeed the 'Satan', as the newly awakened public quickly dubbed her, was to give away time on handicap to every other yacht in the class. Because of her length she was at her best, like *Britannia*, in heavy weather, but she was often a devil to steer and particularly hard to get off the wind.

The Muir Challenge Cup was for amateur helmsmen. As *Satanita* charged down towards the start of the race it became obvious that she was not fully under control, and she narrowly missed a small sailing boat, swamping her with her wake as she passed and knocking one of her crew into the water. Regardless of the rules, the full weight of *Satanita*'s professional skipper was added to that of the man on her tiller ropes, but a yacht of 90ft (27m) waterline can often have its own ideas and in spite of her rudder being held right across her the great cutter would not yield, and carrying on she ran straight into the *Valkyrie*.

The following is an account of the incident told by a witness at the time:

All eyes were centred on *Britannia* who had broken the line first. She was closely followed by the American yacht *Vigilant*, visiting this country for the regatta season, and had tacked inshore to get on *Vigilant*'s weather. Meantime *Valkyrie*, which had been reaching for the start, had just attained a capital position when her progress was rudely interrupted by the extraordinary movement of *Satanita*.

This boat was running down on the port tack but as *Valkyrie* had the right of the road she was kept straight, and it was evident that *Satanita* was going to have to avoid her. However, one of the spectator craft seemed to be in the way, and *Satanita*'s helm was put about strongly to keep clear. This she managed to do, but there was no room left for her to get round the stern of the *Valkyrie*, and loud shouts came from the surrounding boats as a collision seemed inevitable. The helmsman shouted to *Valkyrie* to abandon all rules and save themselves, but his cry was too late. A moment later *Satanita* crashed into *Valkyrie* amidships, striking her with tremendous force slightly abaft the main mast.

Both vessels then locked together, their riggings getting completely mixed up. They hugged each other for a couple of minutes and matters were made worse by *Valkyrie*'s main boom gybing. This almost tore the topmast out of Lord Dunraven's cutter. Ultimately *Valkyrie* got free of *Satanita*, but, being by now a helpless wreck, she bore down on the s.s. *Vanduara*. Besides carrying away several yards of that steam yacht's rails, and completely smashing her small launch, she cut up her planked deck with as much ease as a cheese knife.

Valkyrie appeared now to be settling down, as much water continued to rush into her cabin. Some of her crew scrambled on board the *Vanduara*, but in her death throes she fell back again and cannoned into another steam yacht, the s.s. *Hebe*, whose men snatched the noble Earl from *Valkyrie*'s helm.

The vicinity of the collision was now studded with sailors' heads bobbing in the sea, most of them in south-westers, as there was a heavy mist hanging over the Firth. However, they did not all seem anxious to be picked up, preferring to look towards the yacht they had just left. Interviewed later on coming ashore it was discovered that one of their number, Jack Brown, having been knocked overboard by the force of the collision, had been crushed between the *Vanduara* and the *Valkyrie*, but attempts to save him had failed.

Although the *Valkyrie* sank in deep water, she was later raised, but not before Lord Dunraven had commissioned a third *Valkyrie* to race for the America's Cup of September 1895. From the outset, with the Clyde incident fresh on his mind, the Earl was worried by the huge fleet of boats carrying an estimated fifty thousand spectators, and he begged the committee to move the race to less crowded waters. They refused, and having accused the opposition of other unfriendly acts, at the start of the third race Dunraven dropped his flag. It was one of the most unfortunate moments in the history of yacht racing and several years passed before the reputation of British sportsmanship was to be restored in America.

THE FIRTH OF CLYDE

Amongst the finest and most beautiful natural harbours in the world, the Firth of Clyde had become one of the principal sailing areas of the British Isles by the end of the nineteenth century. Approaching from the south west, past the Mull of Kintyre and the towering rock of Ailsa Craig, past Arran and on towards the Kyles of Bute, yachtsmen are always impressed by the wide expanses of deep water, ruffled only where the wind finds a crack in the backdrop of steep green hills beyond.

Fine harbours inspire men to greatness, but the glories of the Sydney opera house or the Golden Gate of San Francisco are not to be found on the Clyde – such adornments are quite unnecessary. Rather it is the fingers of the Firth, not its entrance, that provide a clue to the Clyde's place in yachting history, for there hide the famous shipyards and the dark veins of commerce which continue up-river to Glasgow and to the heart of the industrial North.

It was brass not beauty that brought big yachting to the Clyde, just as it had been in 1830 with the formation of the Royal Northern Yacht Club. Vast accumulations of wealth found new outlets on the water and later 'Clyde Fortnight', held in early July, became extremely fashionable.

Accident repairs

Incident on the Clyde, 1894

SS Vanduara　　　　　　SS Hebe　　　　　　Valkyrie II　　　　　　Satanita

THE *METEORS*

The Prince of Wales might never have built *Britannia* if it had not been for his impetuous nephew, Kaiser Wilhelm II, Emperor of Germany. In 1892 the Kaiser had mysteriously bought the cutter *Thistle* in order to race her against the best of the British fleet, and the Prince's old cutter *Formosa* was obviously no match for her. In 1887 *Thistle* had competed without success against *Volunteer* for the America's Cup, but she was a fine yacht with a good record. The Kaiser renamed her *Meteor*, but because at that time Germany had few yachtsmen, he manned her entirely with a British crew.

'He was small and short, handsome, with clear blue eyes, a well-set-up little person', wrote Brooke Heckstall-Smith, who knew the Kaiser well. 'He was a little stunted in the neck and a little lop-sided owing to his left arm being shorter than the other. He was exceedingly dramatic and obviously very vain.' The Prince did not like his nephew and, thoroughly mistrusting his intentions, decided to take the Kaiser on at his own game.

It seemed that the Kaiser's motives for entering the yachting scene were entirely political. A previous visit to Cowes during regatta week must have left him with a deep impression, for, in spite of all the distractions presented by the cares of State, and the supervision of a vast army, which he insisted on undertaking himself, he was determined to pursue a sport which he knew little or nothing about. Most Germans lived too far inland to bother about the sea, but the Kaiser thought otherwise. His intention was not merely to buy foreign vessels and man them with foreign crews, but to set up training schools for seamen, persuade the Hamburg merchants and wealthy shipping magnates to build yachts themselves, and turn Germany into a great maritime power.

Launched the following year, *Britannia* soon dealt with the elderly *Meteor*, but she had whetted the Kaiser's appetite and fired his increasing jealousy of the Prince of Wales, 'Uncle Bertie'. In 1896, therefore, he asked George Watson, *Britannia*'s designer, to draw him a new *Meteor* with a larger sail plan than *Britannia*, and in her first season, armed with an extra 2,000sq ft (186sq m) of canvas, *Meteor II* was to win every race she entered.

The Kaiser's domineering and sometimes discourteous nature annoyed his uncle greatly, and it was partly due to this and to a change in the controversial racing rules that caused the Prince of Wales to sell *Britannia* in 1897. 'With her sisters she had been crushed out of the sport by a Kaiser's intrusions and the maladroit legislation of the rule-makers', stated John Irving in his book *The King's Britannia*.

Kaiser Wilhelm II

Meanwhile yacht racing in Germany had become firmly established, and wishing to enhance his reputation, although he still knew precious little about yachting, the Kaiser took *Meteor II* to Kiel. There on the Baltic in 1900 she was soundly thrashed by the British yacht *Sybarita* sent purposely to 'lower her colours', and in the following year she was turned over to the Imperial Navy under the name of *Orion*.

Meteor III, due to the Kaiser's growing resentment of the British, was therefore built in America. Although still crewed largely by British sailors with a British captain, she steadily increased her percentage of Germans aboard, as did the many other yachts, such as *Rainbow*, renamed *Hamburg*, that had passed into German hands. *Meteor III* spent most of her days racing on the Baltic and her success, as the Kaiser decreed, was in establishing Kiel as a rival to Cowes, and Germany as an acknowledged seafaring nation.

By 1909, his long apprenticeship concluded, the Kaiser decided to commission a fourth *Meteor*, to be built by Krupp at Kiel and to be entirely crewed by his own countrymen. Designed by Max Oerst, she was a splendid yacht of 400 tons, and although subsequently often beaten by the great American schooner *Westward*, she played an important part in the British and German regattas until 1913, when for a short time *Meteor V* took over.

Meteor IV's heyday concurred with the magnificent pageant of the Kiel Regatta of 1912. In that summer the Kaiser had raised German yachting to its highest pinnacle and visiting cutters, schooners, yawls and ketches were gathered from France, Italy, Spain, Norway, Great Britain and America. Kiel Week, held every June and hosted by the Imperial Kiel Yacht Club, founded by the Kaiser himself in 1891, was intended to become the premier international yachting event in Europe. But somehow that year, despite the brass bands and the grand receptions, the naked display of German dreadnoughts and battleships, submarines and destroyers made the competitors feel distinctly uncomfortable. The rattling in the rigging had become the rumblings of war.

In many ways for the Kaiser and his *Meteors* the establishment of a German yachting tradition had been a remarkable achievement, but later, when the conflict was over and the Kaiser was languishing in exile, it seemed for a time that German yachting was only a shadowy memory, shattered beyond repair.

THE *HOHENZOLLERN*

Constructed in 1893 by the Vulcan Shipbuilding Company to German Admiralty design, the German Emperor's *Hohenzollern* was for many years one of the most powerful steam yachts in the world. But her bell-mouthed funnels and 'ram' bow, adorned with an imperial double eagle, made her look surprisingly aggressive, and her silhouette was much more that of a warship than that of a lady of state. The huge cost of building her, it was said, had so alarmed the Reichstag that they had cast her with a double role, but those that knew her imperial owner better surmised that she would in any case have been designed that way.

Only in 1913, when she became outclassed by larger royal yachts, did the Kaiser consider changing *Hohenzollern*. Her presence, meanwhile, at Cowes, flying the German Imperial Standard, or at Kiel, sometimes escorted by a zeppelin, was always most impressive. She was the perfect vehicle for the Kaiser's grand aspirations, and a magnificent support vessel for his famous racing yachts.

Meteor IV, carrying a cloud of canvas, seen racing during the memorable Kiel Week of 1912, escorted by warships and the imperial yacht *Hohenzollern*

Imperial Yacht Hohenzollern

Meteor IV

German warship

WESTWARD

No yacht aroused greater envy in the German Emperor's eyes than the magnificent schooner *Westward*. Launched in 1910 from the famous Herreshoff yard on Rhode Island, she was an outstanding example of their superb craftsmanship and the largest sailing yacht in waterline length that they had ever built.

Westward was commissioned by the New York businessman Alexander S. Cochran, and was constructed of the finest materials then available. Her sails, imported from England, were by Ratsey & Lapthorn, and her masts of Oregon pine were so massive that her mainmast when fully rigged weighed 4 tons. But Cochran's master stroke was to engage Captain Charles Barr, the most accomplished helmsman in America, and as soon as *Westward* was fitted out Charlie, as he was known, persuaded her owner to try his new yacht against the best competition that could be found.

The chosen 'killing ground' was Kiel Regatta, and arriving via England in mid-June *Westward* immediately attracted the Kaiser's attention. At that time the Kaiser was exhorting his fellow Germans to snap up every good yacht they could lay their hands on and having patronised George Watson and the well-known American A. Cary Smith, designer of *Meteor III*, he would have given his eyeteeth to acquire such a superb Herreshoff schooner.

During July, with the battle well under way, *Westward* was involved in an incident with *Meteor III*, renamed *Nordstern*. The Kaiser was watching every move, and German skippers knew it, so when the *Nordstern*, bearing down to the start on the port tack, failed to give way to *Westward* on the starboard tack, the Regatta Committee, as usual, turned a blind eye.

Westward swept all before her at Kiel, ultimately giving away an allowance of twenty-five minutes to *Nordstern*, ten minutes to *Meteor IV*, and over seven minutes' handicap to the rest of the competition. It was not very different when she arrived back at Cowes, and during her first season, although she started in no more than eleven open races, she won all of them. But in January the following year, Charlie Barr suddenly died, and shortly afterwards the saddened Cochran put his lovely *Westward* on the market. It seemed that the Kaiser had not long to wait for her to fall into his lap, but it was not until October 1912 that her new owners the Norddeutschen Regatta Verein berthed her back at Kiel, where she was smothered in black paint and renamed *Hamburg II*.

After World War I the great schooner was bought by a London financier, Clarence Hatry, who, christening her *Westward* again, brought her back onto the British

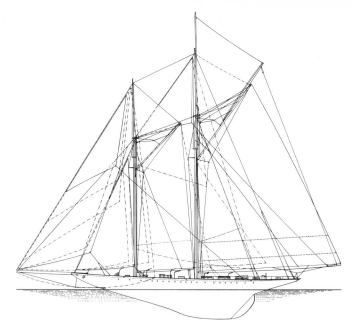

racing circuit. But *Westward* was not to be long with the fleet, for in 1924 Hatry's financial empire was to collapse in the gathering storm, and surprisingly charged with fraud he was sent to gaol for fourteen years. It seemed that *Westward*'s days were also numbered but for her final love affair with Thomas Benjamin Davis.

The son of a fisherman, Davis, after a spell in the British Navy, had made his fortune with his own stevedoring business, loading ships' cargoes in Africa. *Westward* was always his dream boat, and having saved her from a sticky end in the Southampton mud and restored her to her former glory, he raced and cruised in her widely.

TB, as he was affectionately called, would think nothing of shinning up *Westward*'s masts to adjust her rigging, and he was a genius at taking her into port under full sail. Rounding into the wind he would shout blasphemies at some helpless harbour master as the chain rattled out in his and not the harbour master's chosen anchorage. But little did he know that it was they who were to have the last laugh.

In 1942 he died in South Africa aged seventy-five, having left a clause in his will, following the example of his great hero King George V, that if none of his family was prepared to take on the old schooner, *Westward* was to be scuttled. Five years passed, but when on 15 July 1947, much to the dismay of the British public, she was towed out of Dartmouth in thick fog to be sunk by explosive charges somewhere off the Skerries, her huge anchor chain was conveniently taken by the harbour master to secure the moorings of other yachts to follow after her.

In a strong quartering wind some said that *Westward* was unbeatable, but she was such a well balanced yacht that even when reaching she could be steered with ease by Marjorie Davis, the young daughter of her last and most extrovert owner

---

CAPTAIN CHARLES BARR

Like so many of the famous sailing skippers, Charlie Barr was a larger than life character. Born in Scotland at Gourock in 1864, and later resident in the United States, Charlie was a dapper little man with a magnificent waxed moustache, which later became his trade mark of success. Sir Thomas Lipton must have hated the sight of that moustache more than most people, and indeed if Charlie had not met a premature end, he would no doubt have haunted Lipton for all thirty-one years of his involvement in the America's Cup.

The man, it was said, that Charlie had the greatest respect for was Commodore John Pierpoint Morgan, at one time the most influential man in America, and it was he who was largely responsible for Charlie's rise to stardom. In 1899 he hired Charlie to helm *Columbia* against Lipton's challenger *Shamrock I*, and although many reckoned that *Shamrock* was the faster boat, all agreed that it was Charlie's skill which won the day. The story was the same in 1901, and this time *Columbia* beat *Shamrock II* after some of the most hard-fought finishes in the cup's history. But perhaps Charlie's most memorable command was that of the mighty *Reliance* when she successfully defended the cup against *Shamrock III* in 1903. Under his control he now had a vast crew of Scandinavians working both above and below decks, and his victory in a yacht which carried more canvas than any single sticker in history, was a personal triumph.

Charlie's other great moment was when in 1905 he set up the transatlantic record with the American schooner *Atlantic*, a record which amazingly still stands for a monohull. In many ways he was a genius, sought after by owners of many of the finest vessels afloat.

His last command, aged forty-seven, of the beautiful Herreshoff schooner *Westward*, was perhaps his happiest, and when after her first victorious racing season he died suddenly of a heart attack, the yachting world mourned the loss of its most distinguished sailor.

Westward

THE MIGHTY *RELIANCE*

The yacht which was to have as much influence on the design of future racing boats as any was the 1903 America's Cup defender, the mighty *Reliance*. From the tip of her bowsprit to the end of her boom *Reliance* was more than 200ft (61m) long, yet she was less than 90ft (27m) on the waterline. She was the most extreme yacht ever raced, and also, many pointed out, one of the most unseaworthy.

From 1886 onwards there had been an endless battle raging over the rating rules, and by the end of the century, because beam had been left out of the magic formula and only the waterline mattered rather than overall length, designers were opting for light displacement hulls with immense overhangs. As speed is relative to the length of any boat on the water, these long overhangs helped considerably when the yacht was heeling over, but in a light breeze they could also be disadvantageous, causing a certain amount of 'slamming'.

Nat Herreshoff, on being commissioned by a number of New York businessmen to build *Reliance*, had exploited the rules to the limit. She carried an amazing 16,160sq ft (1,501sq m) of sail, no less than twice the area of the later 'J' class and many times greater than the humble 1,800sq ft (167sq m) of the average 12 Metre. Her mainsail, the largest ever made, required well over a ton of Egyptian cotton, and her mast soared 175ft (53m) into the air. Herreshoff had

built *Reliance*, like a fighter plane, out of the lightest possible materials stitched onto web frames. She was thinly plated with bronze and had an aluminium deck with special light-weight gear to give her every possible advantage. Indeed she was so crammed full of new ideas that a few still survive today.

One feature that died with her was her most unusual mast. Depending on the strength of the wind, the wooden topmast could be lowered into the hollow steel mainmast by a winch at its base, the whole structure being stepped on a giant steel kelson. It was said later that her mast broke during trials, but this was not so, her topmast 'simply settling too far in the lower ferrule,' a later Herreshoff explained, 'which was quite easily remedied.'

The combination of her mammoth mainsail and her 108ft (33m) boom was too powerful for all but 4in (100mm) manila sheets, and because it was estimated that her total rig weighed almost 40 tons, and there was no wire rope strong enough to hold it, she had to be fitted, for example, with double bobstays at the bow. Many of the halyards and sheets had been led through fairleads below decks, and here several of her sixty-five largely Scandinavian crew worked the sails to perfection.

How poor Tommy Lipton, when he first clapped eyes on her, must have cursed. *Shamrock III* was indeed a beautiful yacht, but it was soon obvious that she had some 2,000sq ft (186sq m) less sail area than her American opponent. At only 4ft (1.2m) shorter in length, she was to be allowed under two minutes'

Reliance on trials before the America's Cup of 1903 passes a marker flag presented by Sir Thomas Lipton. She would heel over on her beam ends in an eight-knot breeze

advantage over a course of thirty miles. It was not enough, and *Reliance* won in three straight races. But although *Reliance* confounded her critics, it was probably only due to the skilled helmsmanship of her skipper Charlie Barr that she finished unscathed. Herreshoff agreed, and with his approval the rules were changed. Then, sentenced to the scrap-yard, and like the delicate butterfly she was, she died.

BOAT SPEED

A hull designed solely for speed, like a crack 12 metre, can have a maximum speed of 1.5 times the square root of the waterline length. An off-shore racing yacht by a top designer will have a maximum between the two. The reason why the maximum speed is a function of the waterline length derives from the wave formation of a yacht going at speed. A shorter yacht has to start coming up the face of a wave sooner than a longer yacht would do. And, of course, as soon as she starts climbing, her speed stops increasing.

Sir Francis Chichester

Side view of Reliance

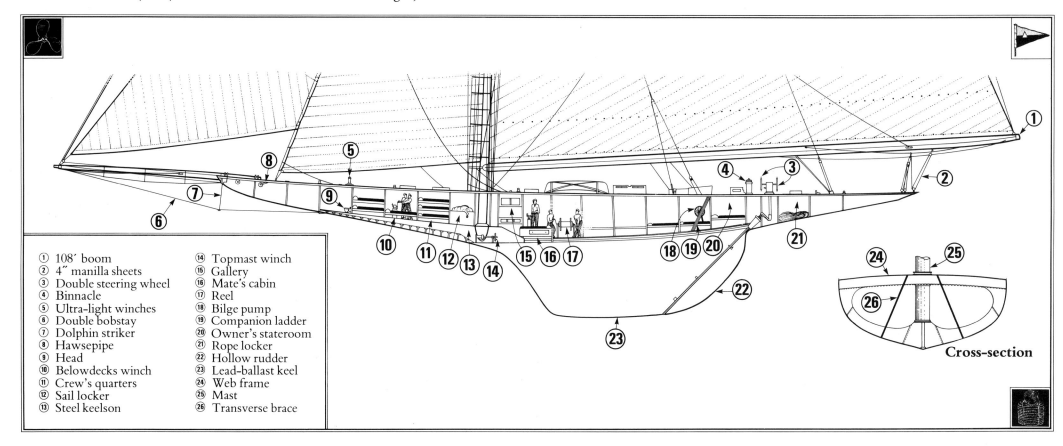

① 108′ boom	⑭ Topmast winch
② 4″ manilla sheets	⑮ Gallery
③ Double steering wheel	⑯ Mate's cabin
④ Binnacle	⑰ Reel
⑤ Ultra-light winches	⑱ Bilge pump
⑥ Double bobstay	⑲ Companion ladder
⑦ Dolphin striker	⑳ Owner's stateroom
⑧ Hawsepipe	㉑ Rope locker
⑨ Head	㉒ Hollow rudder
⑩ Belowdecks winch	㉓ Lead-ballast keel
⑪ Crew's quarters	㉔ Web frame
⑫ Sail locker	㉕ Mast
⑬ Steel keelson	㉖ Transverse brace

Cross-section

Reliance

THE *SHAMROCKS*

The ill feeling created between American and British yachtsmen as a result of the 'Dunraven affair' in 1895 had upset the Prince of Wales (later to be crowned Edward VII) greatly. The Earl's second challenge for the America's Cup had ended at the start of the third race when he had refused to sail across the line – only adding to the already foul air.

As a boy on board the *Victoria and Albert*, Edward had in 1851 watched the crew of *America* salute his mother as the famous yacht sped on to win the race then known as the Hundred Guineas Cup, and he was determined to find a suitable challenger who could put matters right. As luck would have it he found his knight errant in the generous figure of Sir Thomas Lipton.

Born in Glasgow in 1850, young Tommy had left school at the age of ten in order to run errands for a stationery shop. But unhappy with his pay packet he soon found a better job on the Glasgow to Belfast steamers, where he saved enough money (£20) to buy a passage to America. There, aged fourteen, he managed to find work chopping up tobacco on a farm in Virginia, but later moved to a rice plantation in South Carolina, finally stowing away on a ship bound back to New York. His short time there, working in a grocery store, was long enough for him. 'There was an atmosphere in a New York shop, even in those days,' he recalled, 'which seemed to invite trade and to hold it.' Returning to England in 1869 with $500 in his pocket,

Enterprise, the dream ship of Starling Burgess, a leading aeronautical designer, was the most innovative yacht that had ever been built. Her features included a weight-saving duralumin mast and special web frames. Many of her winches were below decks where eight sailors, known as the 'black gang', worked to orders shouted through a hatch

he immediately set about improving his parents' store but, not content, on his twenty-first birthday he opened his own Lipton's, the first of many hundreds of shops to be scattered throughout the British Isles. Lipton's secret of success was marketing, for encouraged by his experience in New York, he set about attracting customers with an advertising campaign the like of which had never been seen. It was therefore not surprising that when he was approached many years later by the Prince of Wales, he was not slow on the uptake.

Lipton, already aged fifty-one, although not perhaps the Royal Yacht Squadron's idea of a yachtsman, was at that time the owner of a fine steam yacht, the *Erin*, and, knowing nothing about sailing, he at once realised the potential for entering a yacht in the world's most prestigious race. If he won, his business would be patronised by more of his countrymen, and if he lost he would become the darling of Americans and sell them twice as much tea.

His first *Shamrock*, designed by William Fife junior and built for the America's Cup of 1899 in great secrecy for 'damn the costs', was sadly not a success. The American designer Nat Herreshoff had produced a fast boat in *Columbia* and she had no difficulty in winning three straight races. So for his second attempt, two years later, he asked George Watson who was later to draw *Britannia*'s lines to do better.

Shamrock II was not a particularly striking vessel and was unfortunate in losing her mast while tuning up in the Solent. She therefore had little time to prepare for the cup and on crossing to America was given the same treatment by *Columbia*, which had again been chosen to defend. The finishes were, however, closer and Lipton, heartened by his boat's performance, decided immediately to give it another try.

His third challenge was issued in 1902, but although Lipton returned to William Fife, who produced the most beautiful yacht that had yet raced for the cup, *Shamrock III* was no match for the mighty *Reliance*, again designed by Nat Herreshoff.

In 1908 Lipton built a fourth *Shamrock* to the 23 Metre International Rule, but it was not until 1913 that he made a further attempt to win the cup when the yacht, which had meanwhile been heading the British first-class racing fleet, was used as a trial horse for the Charles Nicholson designed *Shamrock IV*. Undoubtedly Lipton's most celebrated yacht, 'the ugly duckling' as she was nicknamed was prevented from competing in the cup races set for September 1914 when war broke out while she was still in mid-Atlantic. Lipton could not wait to be fighting his own battles again, so, as soon as the war ended, he refitted his yacht, which had been laid up in New York, and challenged for 1920.

Sir Thomas Lipton

This time, however, the defender *Resolute*, once more designed by the redoubtable Nat Herreshoff, carried less sail, and for a glorious moment Lipton believed that *Shamrock IV* was at last going to 'lift the auld mug'. She finished the first race alone, *Resolute* having carried away her main halyards, and then she won the second. But the third, fourth and fifth races all went to the American. It was a bitter defeat and the closest attempt yet.

To the admiration of the entire sporting world, in 1929 Sir Thomas Lipton, now aged eighty and regarded by many, particularly Americans, as a legend, once more asked Charles Nicholson to build him a yacht to win the America's Cup. *Shamrock V* quickly established a reputation at home by winning fifteen out of her twenty-two first season's races, but nothing could prepare her for the dream ship *Enterprise*, entered by a powerful syndicate headed by Harold S. Vanderbilt, a man with infinitely more resources than himself and a boat which seemed to have everything. *Shamrock* lost all four races and Lipton returned home to die only a few months later, but with the plans for *Shamrock VI* very much on his mind.

No challenger had ever been better prepared than *Shamrock V* to win the America's Cup of 1930. British yachtsmen were so determined that Sir Thomas Lipton should finally 'lift the auld mug' after thirty-one years of extraordinary tenacity that special regattas, starting in June, were organised at Cowes to help *Shamrock V* tune up

SY Erin   *Shamrock V*   *Victoria and Albert*   *Launch carrying Sir Thomas Lipton*

RACING IN TORBAY

'Torbay lies between Hopes Nose and Berry Head, two points bearing from each other N.N.E. and S.S.W. – distant 3½ miles.' So states the channel pilot, which would leave one none the wiser unless referring to the chart.

The oldest yacht club in England, founded around 1770, lies at Starcross in the estuary of the Exe, and in 1811 the *Exeter Flying Post* summoned 'boats carrying no more than 60 yards of canvas' to a match in Torbay. Sheltered from the prevailing south-westerlies, it still is, some would argue, the fairest bay in England for racing yachts and always was, especially in the thirties for the 'Js'.

The Westcountry regattas, often arranged with spectators in mind, will no doubt continue as a fine spectacle, but nothing will ever be quite as magnificent as the Js. There are some who still remember them racing around a triangular course with the sky full of sails, but others recall the committee boat best, a Brixham trawler complete with its ancient starting gun and tattered flags.

'Smoke now wreathed the trawler', one correspondent wrote, 'as in some desperate Napoleonic sea-fight; and it is to be feared that there were moments when the race officials were hard put to it to keep up with the pace of events.' Such was, and still is, the nature of Westcountry people and the delightfulness of their ways.

Amongst the Brixham trawlers ▲

J Class yachts, with *Britannia* in the foreground, racing in Torbay ▶

Endeavour I   *Velsheda*   *Britannia*   *Astra*   *Shamrock V*

THE THIRTIES

VIRGINIA AND THE END OF STEAM

By 1843 the Royal Yacht Squadron, mindful of the Royal Family's interest in steam, decided to amend their rule banning all such enthusiasts from the club. At first they allowed in members with vessels of over 100 tons as long as 'they consumed their own smoke', then, a year later, the minute was changed to: 'No steamer of less than 100 horse-power shall be qualified for admission into, or entitled to the privileges of the Squadron.'

As the attitude towards steam changed, the yachts themselves became more numerous, although many of the great auxiliaries, such as Lord Brassey's *Sunbeam*, were still inclined, when sailing or in port, to hide away their funnels by collapsing them on deck. By the turn of the century, partly due to the development of more efficient engines which issued less smoke, out and out steam yachts began to take over, but in Great Britain they were never to catch on as much as they did in America, nor did British engines ever match their American counterparts for speed.

Virginia Courtauld

VIRGINIA COURTAULD

I only remember Virginia as a very old somewhat eccentric lady living in a rambling colonial house near Umtali in Zimbabwe where she employed, it was estimated, one hundred gardeners. In the hall was a montage of the *Virginia*, cleverly done with glass. Apparently she had fallen very much in love with the *Virginia* from the time she had launched her, and always entertained on her lavishly in her spacious rooms, furnished with unique contemporary designs. My father told me how dangerous it was to take her hospitality for granted, for one evening when she was greeting guests he had almost lost a finger to her not so tame lemur, Mah Jongg, which threatened all those who came on board.

There was one occasion on a cruise to the eastern Mediterranean when, expecting to return from Athens or Istanbul by car, the Stephen Courtaulds instructed their chauffeur Moore to drive out and meet them there with the Mercedes. After driving for many adventurous days through the Balkan States, he arrived exactly on time to be told: 'Moore, we shall not be requiring you as we shall now be returning in the *Virginia*.' 'Very good Sir', said Moore, and without further ado he drove all the way back to London.

But I believe that the most fascinating thing about Virginia was that when she stood on the companionway of the yacht it was noticeable that she had a python tattooed all the way up the inside of her leg!

The Author

Life aboard these yachts in their heyday must have been a very special experience: sitting in wicker chairs under the striped awnings, listening to the rhythmic thump of the pistons and the hissing steam; the steward dodging cinders from the funnel with his tray of cocktails and then lunch below in a panelled dining room, rich with the aroma of cigars. But it was a life reserved for men of great wealth, the running costs of a yacht of about 1,000 tons in 1910 unlikely to be less than £50,000 a year.

With the advent of the diesel engine at the outbreak of World War I it was soon appreciated what immense advantages it would give a yacht over the many problems associated with steam. There would be no more bulky boilers or stokeholds to contend with and the new compact machinery would allow for a great deal more room. During the war most of the steam yachts on both sides of the Atlantic had either been turned over to the Navy by their owners or subsequently commandeered. It was yet another nail in their coffin, and as income tax started to bite harder and stocks began their tumble in 1928 the golden era of the steam yacht came almost to an abrupt end.

One British steam-yacht designer who had stood head and shoulders above the rest was George Watson, also famous in the sailing world. In 1929, when the horizon was looking distinctly foggy, he was approached by Major Stephen Courtauld who asked him to design a twin-screw diesel yacht, which he was to name after his wife *Virginia*. Launched in May 1930, she was 209ft (64m) overall with a 29ft (9m) beam and had a displacement of 712 tons. Few will deny that with her clipper bow, long overhanging stern, raking masts and funnel, and her topgallant fo'c'sle she had the most pleasing lines reminiscent of his former steam yachts, but Watson had designed her to be a great deal more efficient. Her two Gardner diesel engines, almost vibration free, drove her along at a cruising speed of around fourteen knots, and large enough fuel tanks had been installed to enable the yacht to cross the Atlantic in both directions without any need for stopping.

Many of her early cruises were on the beautiful waters of the west coast of Scotland. An account from *The Firth of Clyde* by George Blake reads: 'There were few of these darlings left after the First World War. Sir Thomas Lipton's famous *Erin* had gone down in the Mediterranean, and many more fine ships had been casualties of the bread-and-butter economies then blighting the world. By 1936 Lord Inchcape's *Rover*, Major Courtauld's *Virginia*, and Lady Yule's notorious yacht *Nahlin*, were the only sizeable yachts left that really come to mind.' On one occasion off Hunter's Quay, *Virginia*'s fast Thorneycroft launch ran a big end, and a mechanic was sent all the way to Scotland to repair it, a service unlikely to be available today.

Virginia also cruised widely in other countries, her longest trip being to the islands of Indonesia. During World War II she served with distinction as a hospital ship, later becoming the property of Lord Camrose. What eventually became of her no one really knows, but it is said that she now lies off Freetown, Sierre Leone, passing her sunset years as a floating casino.

MY *Virginia* off Cowes in 1935 before attending the Naval Review

M.Y. Virginia

THE LONE *RANGER*

My mast is duralumin, but costlier than Gilt
The wind that fills my riggin' is a million dollar breeze
From my bowsprit to my topsail, I am wholly
    Vander-built.
And I only go a-sailing in the most exclusive seas.
                                                    Redbook, 1937

Ranger may have been born with a silver spoon, but
when she was conceived it did not seem like it. Times
were hard in America in 1937, even for those with deep
enough pockets, and when Harold S. Vanderbilt, great
grandson of The Commodore, tried to get together a
syndicate to meet Sir T. O. M. Sopwith's challenge for
the America's Cup, nobody came forward. Feeling,
possibly, a little peeved by the attitude of his fellow
countrymen, but himself eager for the fray, Vanderbilt
put *Ranger* out to tender, which was duly won by the
Bath Iron Works in Maine, the first time an America's
Cup defender had not been built by the Herreshoff
yard in Bristol, Rhode Island, for almost forty years.
Because of dwindling orders, they had agreed to build
Ranger virtually at cost. To cut the bill further,
Vanderbilt used many of the fittings from the 1930 and
1934 cup winners, *Enterprise* and *Rainbow*, but no
expense was spared on her design, once again the re-
sponsibility of ex-aircraft designer Starling Burgess,
although he agreed to a much reduced fee.

Ranger's mast

(*Left*) The New York Yacht Club burgee; (*right*) the signal of
Britain's Royal Yacht Squadron

This time, however, Vanderbilt had asked Burgess
to share the task with the brilliant young Olin
Stephens, and each was invited to present two drawings. These were then made into wax models, and after
the first attempt at tank testing in yachting history, the
best, and also as it turned out the most radical, design
was chosen – to remain a closely guarded secret. The
total cost of the *Ranger* campaign was later estimated
to have been in the region of $500,000, of which
approximately $180,000 had been spent on building
her. Compared with the estimated $900,000 spent on
Enterprise in 1930 it was undoubtedly a snip.

The most innovative features on *Ranger* were probably her duralumin mast and her non-stretch rod
rigging. Launched on 11 May 1937 with great ceremony, it was decided to step the beautiful mast before
she was taken south to Marble Head for the races. It
proved to be an expensive mistake. On the voyage,
while being towed by 'Mike' Vanderbilt's motor yacht
Vara, the rod rigging started working loose and during
the night, first length by length, and then frighteningly
fast, the whole $15,000 rig came crashing to the deck.
It could have been a bad omen, but it did not turn out
that way. In a few days *Ranger* proudly carried a new
stick, and from it she was to fly a huge spinnaker of
18,000sq ft (1,672sq m), or two-fifths of an acre, the
largest sail ever made.

The most noticeable features about the new American
defender, however, were her snubbed-off almost
rounded bow, and her long overhanging stern. In no
way a beautiful yacht, she would squat down as if to
achieve increased waterline length and give an
immense impression of power. And *Ranger* was
powerful; Vanderbilt called her his 'super J'. Somehow
she had a magic quality, a mixture of cleverly planned
features that together made her fly like the wind. On
one occasion in the cup races to follow she was to sail
fifteen miles to windward in just two hours three
minutes.

Such was her dominance in 1937 that *Endeavour II*,
which had arrived to challenge her for the Cup, complete with her older sister, never stood a chance. In the
first race *Endeavour* was beaten by seventeen minutes,

and in the second race by eighteen. By the fourth race
there was hardly a spectator left, and so complete was
her defeat that Sopwith could do little else but marvel
at the winner. 'Unbelievable', he said, 'quite unbelievable', and Charles Nicholson, *Endeavour*'s designer, could do little but accept that *Ranger*'s lines
were 'the most revolutionary advance in hull design in
half a century.' Mike Vanderbilt had little to add. 'She
was', he said a year later, 'the ultimate conception.'

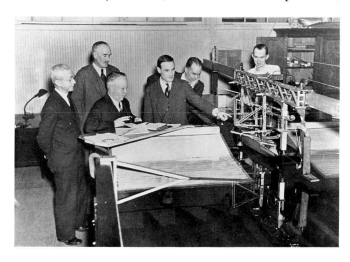

TANK TESTING

Although the practice had been applied previously to
steamships, tank testing had not been part of yacht design until the technique was pioneered by Professor
Kenneth Davidson of the Stevens Institute of Technology in New Jersey, and first used on *Ranger*. The
difficulty with yachts was that they had different
angles of attack, and a machine had to be invented
which could test the designs when heeling over.

After *Endeavour* had lost the America's Cup series
in 1934, Tommy Sopwith had, somewhat rashly,
handed her plans to Starling Burgess, and now he was
to make good use of them. Americans had little doubt
that on that occasion the British yacht was the faster,
the situation only being saved at the last minute by the
USA's much respected second helmsman, Sherman
Hoyt. Determined not to let this happen again, Professor Davidson carefully analysed her shape for heel and
yaw, pitch and drag, in every way possible.

Although the question of who designed *Ranger*'s
hull, Stephens or Burgess, remained a secret for over
twenty years, eventually it leaked out that it was the
professor who had been asked to make the final
decision and that the winning design was by Starling
Burgess.

The lone *Ranger*, the best and last of the Js, and a yacht which
stood out on her own

Ranger   *Endeavour II*

CRUISING IN GREAT BRITAIN – THE YACHT *DUET*

The first cruising club in Great Britain, later known as the Royal Cruising Club, had been formed by a lawyer from Lincoln's Inn in 1880, and this had been followed by two other bodies only concerned with cruising, the Cruising Association and the Clyde Cruising Club. But cruising did not really come into its own as such until the period between the wars, particularly in the 1930s.

The word cruising was probably derived from the Dutch word *kruisen* meaning to cross, and from it the naval word cruiser, a ship of the line which tacked back and forth when on patrol. But the word was often interpreted differently by different clubs and at different times. Generally cruising means to visit other places and staying on board overnight, but in 1954 the Ocean Cruising Club was formed, which ruled that members must accomplish an offshore passage in a boat no longer than 70ft (21m) over a distance of not less than 1,000 miles.

One of the first to approve of the new club was the arctic explorer Augustine Courtauld. In July 1930 he set out on his third journey to Greenland with thirteen others on the *Quest*, the ship on which Shackleton had sailed on his last expedition and died, now crewed by Norwegians. As they sailed out from St Katharine's Dock, they stopped for a brief farewell on Stephen Courtauld's *Virginia*, and Percy Lemon, the expedition's signals officer, was bitten so hard by the ship's lemur (see page 44), that he had bled all over the upper deck.

Today, travelling between Europe and the United States, we fly over the Arctic in comparative comfort, but in 1930 it was still only planned on paper. The British Arctic Air-route Expedition, led by a remarkable man Gino Watkins and run by a committee headed by the Prince of Wales, had set out with the purpose of following the proposed route and taking important weather recordings through the darkness of the arctic winter. During August the expedition established a weather station high on the Greenland ice-cap, but none appreciated the fearsome conditions to come. When in December the third relief party set out to occupy it they took six weeks instead of the normal six days to get there, and finding themselves desperately short of rations, rather than abandon the station, Courtauld volunteered to sit it out alone. During the five months that he was destined to be there, virtually buried alive, two plans kept him sane; the first for getting engaged and the second for designing the best cruising yacht in the world.

The order in which he placed these ambitions is a matter for conjecture, but when, after his safe return he found his dream yacht *Gaviota* and his bride at the same time, he renamed the yacht *Duet*, and in 1932 took them both cruising on the Clyde.

In 1934 Courtauld sailed *Duet* to Holland where she competed in a race to Copenhagen against one yacht crewed by German submarine officers with orders from Hitler to win. Later, while sailing in the Solent, she was almost run down by the great schooner *Westward*. 'At last, when there seemed a mere matter of inches to go', Courtauld wrote, 'a voice sang out from for'ard, "Luff sir, for God's sake, luff." Her steersman moved the helm one spoke: *Westward*'s boom drew in a foot, and she rushed by.'

Following several cruises to the lovely shores of Brittany, in 1939 Courtauld sailed to Bergen in Norway, but this was to be her last trip until the war was over, which she fortunately survived unscathed. After further cruising, mainly in Scotland, *Duet*'s next challenge was a voyage to Jamaica. Setting out from Teignmouth, she encountered a severe storm in the Bay of Biscay, and had to make for Corunna to undergo repairs. When Courtauld found that they did not have enough cash to pay the extortionate bill, the Spanish placed a guard on the boat, but, following in the traditions of his buccaneering forebears, he had the guard dumped ashore and set out again into the teeth of the storm.

Courtauld's last cruise in *Duet* was in 1955. Sadly he had become gravely ill but, although confined to a wheelchair, he sailed her down to Majorca with his family. When he died four years later, *Duet* was lent by his son Christopher to the Ocean Youth Club, who still win prizes with her in the Tall Ships race.

AUGUSTINE COURTAULD EMERGING FROM THE TENT AFTER FIVE MONTHS ALONE

The weather station on the Greenland ice-cap consisted of a 10ft (3m) diameter domed tent with a high ventilator tube, and two igloos connected to it by tunnels under the snow. At first life was not too unpleasant except for frostbite in his toes, but after a time, with blizzards gusting at up to 120mph, Courtauld began finding it hard to dig his way out to read the instruments which he was required to do six times a day.

On one occasion he recorded the lowest ever temperature of 90°F (62°C) below freezing, but eventually he became completely snowed in and had to give up the unequal struggle in order to survive. His friends had left him on 6 December and at the end of April lit his last candle, writing in his diary: 'I trust in God absolutely. I am sure He does not wish me to die alone.' One by one his stores had run out, and on 5 May, the day the fourth search party finally found him, his primus flickered for the last time. 'Are you there Courtauld?' Watkins shouted down the ventilator, which was all that was visible. 'Yes', a voice, amazingly, replied.

> The power of man is as his hopes
> In darkest night, the cocks are crowing.
> With the sea roaring and the wind blowing;
> Adventure. Man the ropes.
>
> John Masefield

This poem, carved on polished wood and taken by Courtauld to Greenland, is still secured above the chart table on *Duet*.

Reunion with the *Quest* in the Thames Estuary. Courtauld was president of the Cruising Association until his untimely death in 1959 (Sketch for an oil painting on sepia paper)

DUET (ex *Gaviota*).

A gaffrigged yawl of 22 tons. T.M.
Described in 1913 edition of Dixon, Kemp.

Dimensions
Length overall, 50 feet   Sail area 1,652 sq. ft.
Length on water line, 38 feet   (plain sail)
Beam 11.1 feet   Sailmaker—Cranfield &
Draught, 6.5 feet   Carter.
R.O.R.C. rating—32.80'

Building
By Whites at Southampton in 1912.
Designed by Linton Hope to Lloyds Class 18AC.

Construction
Keel—of English Elm in one piece with nine and a half tons lead keel, through bolted with one inch yellow metal bolts.
Stem, Sternpost, Deadwood, Rudder—English Oak, well seasoned.
Rudder Hangings—Yellow Metal straps, through bolted.
Rudder Trunk—Teak, watertight.
Frames—Selected English oak, spaced twenty-two inches with American Rock Elm bent timbers in between each frame.
Stringer—Teak, through bolted to every frame.
Floors—Wrought Iron, galvanized.
Horn Frames—Oak, through bolted to sternpost and deck head. Centre piece of teak bolted to archboard.
Archboard—Teak.
Shelf—Teak.
Beams—Oak, dovetailed on top of shelf.
Carlings—With all necessary mast and capstan chocks.

Duet

Quest

THE NEW YORK YACHT CLUB CRUISE

Just three days after the formation of the New York Yacht Club, at 9 o'clock on 2 August 1844 eight yachts, *Gimcrack*, on which the inaugural meeting had been held, *Spray, La Coquille, Cygnet, Dream, Minna, Petrel* and *Mist* took part in the first cruise to be organised by the committee. The fleet stopped at Huntington on Long Island, then at New Haven, Gardiners Bay and Oyster-Pond Point, arriving at Newport, Rhode Island on the afternoon of 5 August. It was a splendid binge and when the members had sufficiently recovered, they vowed to make it an annual occasion.

The first club house was situated close to New York City at Elysian Fields, Hoboken, and had been generously furnished by John C. Stevens, the first commodore. Subsequently, in 1868, long after he had taken the *America* to England and plundered the Hundred Guineas Cup, the club moved to Staten Island, then to Madison Avenue before occupying its present premises fronting on West Forty-fourth Street in midtown Manhattan. During this period, and encouraged by the summer activities, particularly the cruise, the club increased its membership every year.

Within a comparatively short time the New York Yacht Cruise had become the major event in the American yachting calender. Spanning first a week and then ten days during August, the cruise, starting from home waters, involved passage races from port to port and major regattas at Newport, Rhode Island and sometimes at Marblehead, Massachusetts. Many of the yachts taking part would first sail up Long Island Sound, 'the ideal place', Anthony Heckstall-Smith, the British yachting correspondent, wrote in 1921, 'for any kind of yacht up to a 300 ton schooner. It is a lovely landlocked sea of deep water – ten miles extending to twenty miles in width. Along the shores are little natural harbours, rocky bays and sandy coves, where anybody can drop an anchor for the night. There are sweet woodlands extending in places to the water's edge, and the blue sea is as clean and clear as crystal in the summer sun.'

As the New York Yacht Club had gathered strength, many of its members had expressed a desire to establish stations from Long Island Sound to Martha's Vineyard where yachtsmen could congregate and receive 'proper attention' while taking their recreation. A special committee was appointed, and in July 1892 the first of these 'charming country club-houses' was opened at Bay Ridge, with others quickly following at New York itself, Whitestone, New London, Connecticut, where a splendid building was erected on Pequot Avenue, then at Shelter Island, Newport, Rhode Island, and Vineyard Haven, Massachusetts. The New London station proved particularly convenient, and it was here in the magnificent harbour that the yachts gathered each year for the start of the much looked forward to cruise. Leaving Long Island Sound and Fisher's Island behind, the fleet then sailed into open water, past Block Island and on to the Brenton Reef lightship, marking the narrow entrance to the sheltered bay of Newport, a town famous for its strong naval connections and its summer cottages. Vanderbilt's 'cottage' had been built in 1892 for the staggering sum of $11,000,000, and there were many others, all vying to be that much more fashionable and ostentatious than the rest. In 1937 Newport still remained the holiday playground for the super rich, and the cruise was notable for the entertainment lavished on its seaborne guests. But far more exciting that year was the presence of the Js.

The Js starting on the first leg of the New York Yacht Club Cruise in 1937

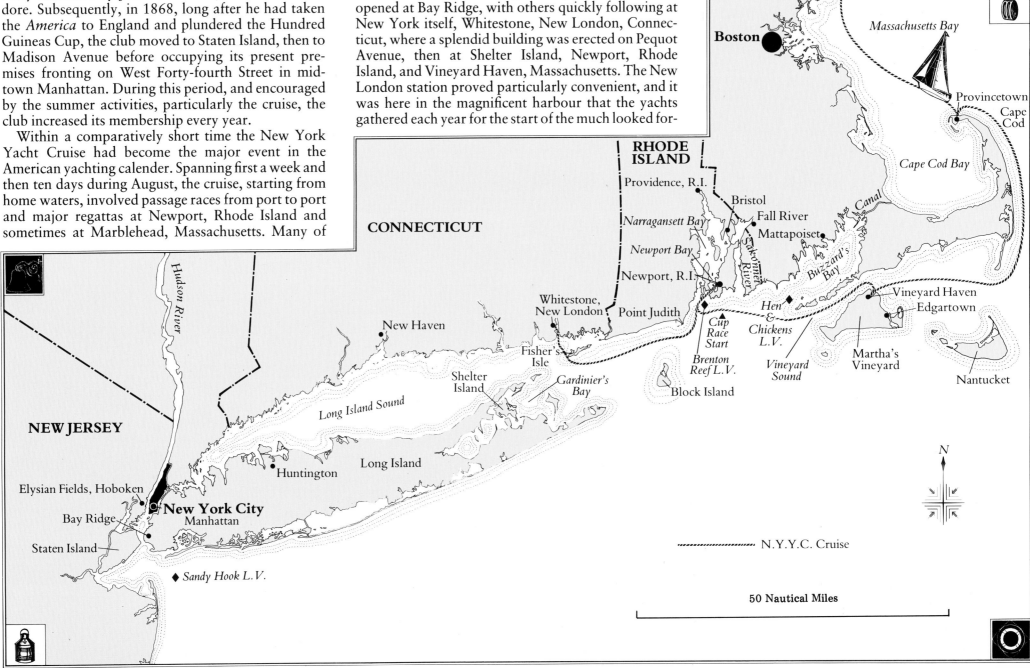

Rainbow   Endeavour I   Yankee   Endeavour II   Ranger

THE OCEAN RACERS

THE 1866 TRANSATLANTIC RACE

The first yacht to cross the Atlantic in either direction was the *America* in June 1851. But although her ambitions stretched far beyond that mighty ocean and she was to win her spurs in a very different hunting ground, later to be known as the America's Cup, her voyage inspired many other countrymen to follow her brave example. The *America* brought an international spirit into yachting that immensely increased the sport's popularity and, apart from the forced interlude of the American Civil War of 1861–5, many vessels both large and small were soon to be sailed east into the Atlantic swell and pitted against the great unknown.

In July 1866 William Hudson had left New York in a boat merely 26ft (8m) long and, crossing the Atlantic in only thirty-five days, he had, although some claimed he had cheated, fired the imagination of the world. One American admirer was James Gordon Bennett, who in 1861 had lorded it over Long Island Sound with two six-pounders and a cannon aboard his yacht *Henrietta*. The war over, he was just beginning to find life a little tame, when one night in a club he overheard his companions, owners of two fine yachts, brag about a transatlantic race. The stakes were to be substantial. 'George and Franklin Osgood bet Pierre Lorillard, Jr., and others $30,000 that the *Fleetwing* can beat *Vesta* to the Needles on the coast of England. Yachts to start from Sandy Hook on the second Tuesday in December, 1866; to sail according to the rules of the New York Yacht Club, waiving the allowance of time.' Although it was then winter, Bennett could not wait to enter.

It was a daring adventure. 'Deep-sea racing is never likely to be a lady's pastime,' wrote one commentator, 'the carrying of sails until the very last moment, the "cracking on" of vast, bellying weights of canvas to pull you through the inky night, the driving through fog and squalls of rain with the temperature dropping 20 degrees on a single watch, seeing your boom crash through the crests of the brimming sea, or the foresails wringing the masthead as one would wring the neck of a flapping fowl: these will be conditions to try the most hardened sailor.' It was not surprising that all three yachts found it difficult to make up a crew.

James Gordon Bennett, who served with the *Henrietta* during the Civil War

On a cool bright day the men, including several expensively hired whaler captains, were cheered away as they boarded the tugs which were to take them out to their yachts. The hills of Staten Island were dotted with observers and flags were flying from every villa as a fleet of pilot boats clustered off West Bank to escort the yachts to sea, while the forts lining the harbour entrance dipped their colours in salute. All three yachts, which were very similarly built, had been carefully equipped for the voyage, each carrying spare sails, spars, wire rigging and extra tillers. So closely had they performed in previous inshore contests that the only prejudice was against *Vesta*, which was fitted with a centreboard, and substantial wagers were laid on the other two. Indeed as the tugs were cast off and the yachts crossed the start almost abeam of each other it seemed as if they were joined together with glue.

Within a few days the weather was blowing its worst and on 18 December *Henrietta*'s doctor noted: 'Just at midnight the yacht was struck by a tremendous sea that burst over her quarter, slapping high up her foresail and staving in the yacht's boat. Simultaneously the carpenter rushed wildly into the owner's cabin, pale with alarm, and shouted "Mr Bennett, we must heave to, she is opening forward, Sir". But nobody stirred except the captain, who after a brief investigation stated quietly, "Mr Brown you should know your bilges".'

At 3am on Christmas day *Henrietta* passed the Lizard light, and when at noon they picked up a Cowes pilot and were told that no other American yacht had passed up the Channel, the crew gave a hearty cheer. She stormed on past the Needles under full canvas to win in 13 days 21 hours and 55 minutes.

After 3,000 miles' racing at the Scilly light, *Vesta*, which subsequently got lost in the fog, had been only ten miles behind, but *Fleetwing*, which eventually finished second, had not been so lucky. Hit by the same gale as reported by *Henrietta*, eight men had been washed out of her open cockpit. Although two were miraculously dumped on board again, it was, and still is, the worse known disaster in the history of transatlantic racing.

The start of the 1866 Transatlantic Race

Henrietta   *Vesta*   *Fleetwing*

ATLANTIC AND THE ATLANTIC

Without question the greatest and most impressive ocean racer of them all was the American auxiliary three-masted schooner *Atlantic*. Designed by William Gardner and built by Townshend and Downey of New York in 1904, during her sixty-five-year reign she changed hands no less than eight times, meeting each new challenge differently but with the confidence of a record holder. Wherever she went *Atlantic* was toasted as the fastest sailing yacht ever to have crossed the 'Pond', and her magnificent feat, accomplished in only her second year afloat, gave her a long-standing aura of respect among yachtsmen that has never been surpassed.

When the great transatlantic race for the German Emperor's Cup was announced in 1905, there was much speculation about which type of sailing vessel would win, the event being open to yachts of any rig, but all knew that it was going to be a severe test of seamanship. The race indeed started in thick fog, from the Sandy Hook lightship at 12.15pm on 17 May. As the gun boomed, the yawl *Ailsa* was first away. During the afternoon the yachts began to separate, some going south on the steamer track and the others taking a more northerly route.

A correspondent on *Endymion*, then the Atlantic record holder, wrote, 'Throughout the night we foamed along with a fresh following breeze and the light weather sails lifting against the misty, moon-lit sky. We were conscious that we were doing well and hoped to leave our long black rival behind in the dark; but daylight showed her away on our port bow after which we lost sight of her.' He was of course referring to the raven-black hull of *Atlantic* which, passing the *Hamburg* late that afternoon, was never again to be sighted during the race by her rivals.

Captain Charlie Barr, at *Atlantic*'s helm, now sailed *Atlantic* unmercifully. 'She is being driven like a frightened bird', entered one passenger in his diary, 'while the following northwesterly rips the sails from her spars and the seas hammer at her sleek hull until every quivering plank seems to scream in protest, our skipper, one hand on the lifeline rigged along the rails, watches the springing masts, studying, calculating speed and strain, and hangs on to his canvas to the very limits of safety.' *Atlantic*'s first owner, Wilson Marshall, and other members of the afterguard pleaded with Charlie to reduce sail, but to no avail – 'Sir, you hired me to win this race in *Atlantic*,' he said, 'and that is what I will do.'

She charged on through mounting seas at an average

RACE
FOR THE
OCEAN CUP

Presented by
His Imperial Majesty the German Emperor

Atlantic on her way to crossing the 'Pond' in 12 days, 4 hours and 1 minute, a record which stood for no less than seventy-five years – until the maxi-multihulls began chipping away at it during the 1980s

of 14.2 knots, on the sixth day sighting an iceberg. 'We passed quite close to this mass of glacial ice,' wrote our diarist. 'Much of it was submerged, but across this frozen shoal the seas were breaking heavily.' The passengers watched in awed silence as she creamed by, her wake soon lost in the following white caps.

Atlantic reached the Bishop's Rock in 11 days, 16 hours, but her hopes of completing the crossing in under 12 days were then dashed by light winds and she took an agonising 12 hours to sail the last 50 miles to the finish off the Lizard. She had beaten her closest rival the *Hamburg* by over a day, had smashed *Endymion*'s time handsomely, and had claimed her place in the record books.

The parting of the ways. Atlantic heads away from Hamburg early in the race

Hamburg   Atlantic   US warships

JOLIE BRISE

In 1912 Alexandre Paris wrote in his notebook. 'From my earlier designs, I knew where I was going, and I drew her very quickly.' The place Le Havre, the vessel *Jolie Brise*. Massively built of 4 x 4in (100mm) Normandy oak timbers, and measuring nearly 50ft (17m) overall, she had been constructed on the lines of a French pilot cutter, but she was even prettier and somewhat wider in the beam.

As soon as she was launched, *Jolie Brise* became embroiled in World War I, but after it was over and she had done her stint escorting ships into the harbour at Le Havre she was bought by one Alain Hervette, and moved to Concarneau for a new life tunny fishing which she did for three seasons, before making history.

It happened that in the spring of 1923 an Englishman, Evelyn George Martin, was visiting France with friends when his practised eye, for he had a passion for working boats, fell upon *Jolie Brise*. Returning later he acquired her for some £300 and sailed her back to Teignmouth (my own home port) in Devon. There, helped by a clever shipwright Sydney Briggs who later became his skipper for a time, she was carefully fitted out as a yacht.

It was true that since 1906 yachts had already been racing annually from Brooklyn to Bermuda and before then they had twice, in 1870 and 1887, raced across the Atlantic, but, inspired by a contributor to *Yachting World*, Martin now set about planning what was to be the first ocean race held on the British side of the 'Pond'.

The Fastnet race, which is now generally considered the most exacting ocean race in the world, was first advertised in the press early in 1925 and was greeted with mixed enthusiasm, although fourteen yachts eventually took part. Starting on 15 August from Ryde on the Isle of Wight, and turning at the Fastnet Rock off the south-west coast of Ireland, it ended at Plymouth, six hundred miles later, in triumph for *Jolie Brise*. So elated was her owner that, as the last yacht neared the finishing line, Martin gathered his fellow competitors at the Royal Western Yacht Club and, with himself voted commodore, they formed the Ocean Racing Club.

In 1923 the Bermuda race had been revived largely as a result of the endeavours of Herbert Stone, then editor of the American magazine *Yachting*, who, working closely with the Ocean Racing Club, agreed that future events should be run on alternate years. In 1926 Martin set sail in *Jolie Brise* for Bermuda in order to compete, 'her full jackyard topsail gleaming white in the westering sun', as *Yachting* reported, returning just

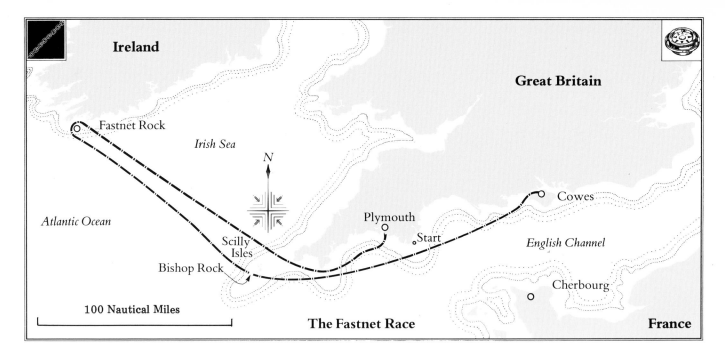

The Fastnet Race

in time for the second Fastnet race, in which she finished fifth.

In the 1929 Fastnet race, *Jolie Brise* was sailed by a new owner, Robert Somerset, ex Eton, Sandhurst and the Grenadier Guards and heir presumptive to the Duke of Beaufort. Then aged thirty-one, he was in a competitive mood, and for the second time she was driven home first over the line. But he was not to use her solely for ocean racing, and during the winter months she would stalk the Devon estuaries and take Somerset and his friends duck shooting.

There was a westerly gale blowing up the Channel for the 1930 Fastnet, but when Somerset asked his skipper, 'What do you think?' Fred Crossley replied, 'She can take it if we can.' And so they sailed on to win again for a third time, *Jolie Brise* thus setting up a record that has never been beaten.

Somerset sailed her back to America again in 1932, and there she saved the crew of the blazing schooner *Adriana* in probably the most dramatic rescue that the Bermuda race has yet seen. *Jolie Brise* was still hitting the headlines but while ocean racing was continuing to develop, her own glorious era was coming to an end. On her return home she was again put on the market and then became a cruising boat, before long covering several thousand miles of the Mediterranean.

During the 1930s both the now Royal Ocean Racing Club and the Cruising Club of America had set about improving their rules, and in 1941 a number of races were combined to form the six-week Southern Ocean Racing Conference (SORC) series centred on Florida and the Bahamas. But it was not until 1945, after the end of World War II that the first long-distance race, from Sydney to Hobart, was held in the southern hemisphere.

Jolie Brise, after a quiet war back in England, was then for a long time sailed as a family boat in Portugal, but in 1977 she was brought back home again and ever since, after a thorough face lift, has lived a life of luxury, still in service, at the Exeter Maritime Museum.

The Pilot's Jetty, Le Havre (Camille Pissarro, 1830–1903)

Lights and Buoys (Merchant Shipping Act 1932). It is an offence to injure, or merely run foul of, and whether by accident or otherwise, any lighthouse, light-vessel, buoy, beacon, etc, or to ride by or make fast to one. Penalty £50, in addition to making good the damage

Fastnet Rock

Jolie Brise

Condor

Nirvana

FLYING ROUND THE WORLD

The tragedy of the 1979 Fastnet race, in which, due to a vicious gale, fifteen men died, was a lesson in seamanship that served ocean racing well. Although many of the larger boats came through almost unscathed, *Condor* smashing the record and *Tenacious*, skippered by Ted Turner, winning on corrected time, it showed that materials were being used in construction that were simply not up to the job. 'There should be some rethinking of priorities aboard racing boats,' wrote Don Graul in *Yachting*. 'To win these days a boat must be sailed at and beyond the edge of safety and survival.'

One yachtsman who was used to roughing it was Cornelis van Rietschoten, who has kindly written the foreword to this book. As a young man in 1947 he had sailed a tiny 'Dragon' with a friend across the North Sea, and ten years after this incredible voyage, he had been dismasted in the Fastnet race of 1957. He soon learned to treat all gear with the greatest suspicion and is now one of the most fastidious sailors around.

The first Whitbread Round the World Race of 1973–4 had appealed to Cornelis' keen sense of adventure, so in 1975 he asked Sparkman & Stephens to design him the 65ft yacht *Flyer*. She was launched in time for the 1977 race, and superbly prepared. The race began on 27 August: on the afternoon of 25 March 1978, almost seven months and 5,220 miles later, she surfed past Cowes in a force 8 gale to beat the fifteen other competitors convincingly, on handicap.

Having won once, the decision to enter a second time in 1981 was all the more difficult, but excited by the opportunity of racing against several other maxis (sloops longer than 70ft), and with support from Prince Bernhard of the Netherlands, Conny ordered *Flyer II* (a 77-footer designed by German Frers and again built by Walter Huisman in Holland).

After four years the race had grown, and twenty-nine yachts crossed the start off Portsmouth on 29 August. *Flyer* was first in Capetown, first to Sydney, first to Rio de Janeiro, and finally first home over the line and first on handicap: altogether an astonishing achievement.

◄ *Condor*, the Ron Holland-designed 80ft maxi, with *Nirvana* in the Sydney–Hobart race, 1983

Flyer II, winner of the 1981/2 Whitbread Race, seen storming through the Southern Ocean ►

Flyer II

EPIC VOYAGES

CHICHESTER AND *GIPSY MOTH IV*

And this sublime solitude is never loneliness; for, on the ocean one is never less alone than when alone, until the first faint whiff of perfume from the land and the muffled sound of distant church bells from a native town.

A sailor

There have now been so many epic voyages across the oceans of the world that it would be hard to list them. However, among the British heroes such as Robin Knox Johnston, who in 1968 completed the first non-stop circumnavigation in his yacht *Suhaili*, and Chay Blyth, who repeated the feat with *British Steel* in 1970 but in the opposite direction and against the prevailing winds, the best remembered voyage is that of Sir Francis Chichester.

Chichester had been a loner for most of his life, and even at Marlborough College he had found it very hard to fit in. In 1918 he told his housemaster that he was leaving, and with £10 in his pocket, he boarded a cargo ship bound for New Zealand. His initial job in Wel-

As the cyclonic winds, ripping through the southern hemisphere, are forced by the great barrier of the Andes over the shelving seas which beat against the bleak black rock of Cape Horn, they sometimes crest at over 100ft (30m), higher than most seven-storey buildings

lington was as a shepherd earning 10s a week, but later he joined a successful estate agency. One of the partners was a man called Goodwin, and it was he who started Chichester on his first notable career of flying.

Having acquired the agency for A. V. Roe, they bought two Avro Avians, hired pilots for them, and then set out on a barnstorming tour of New Zealand. Inevitably Chichester thought that he could fly the machines better himself, but after nearly nineteen hours of instruction he was still not flying solo. He returned to England to see his family, won his licence at Brooklands and bought himself a little Gipsy Moth biplane.

In 1929 only one man had ever flown solo from England to Australia; however, the intrepid Chichester set out for Sydney. 'Rich Young Man's Amazing Flight' was the headline in the *Daily Mail* on 21 December, but most of his savings had already gone.

Chichester arrived in Sydney to a rousing reception on 19 January 1930, and after a brief rest, decided to attempt the first ever flight from east to west across the Tasman Sea. After shipping his plane back to New Zealand, he fitted her with floats, and then, navigating with a sextant, he crossed the fifteen hundred miles of water, stopping only at two tiny islands on the way. Unfortunately, however, triumph was to turn to disaster for, deciding afterwards to return to England via Japan, he flew into a high tension cable over the Japanese coast and crashed into a harbour wall, breaking no less than thirty bones.

Gipsy Moth IV nears Plymouth at the end of her voyage

His interest in sailing began only in 1953 when he bought a small boat which he renamed *Gipsy Moth II*. She was soon followed by *Gipsy Moth III*, but on being told that he had meanwhile developed lung cancer he set out to conquer the disease by winning the 1960 transatlantic race, and two years later by recording the fastest ever Atlantic crossing single handed. No sooner had he landed than he started planning what he called his 'round the world ambition,' the greatest exploit of them all.

The 54ft (16.5m) *Gipsy Moth IV*, purpose built by Camper & Nicholson, was launched in March 1966 by Sheila, Chichester's long-suffering wife, and on 27 August he crossed the start off Plymouth Hoe, heading for the Cape of Good Hope. At heart a great romantic, his intention was to beat the wool clippers round the globe, with just one stop at Sydney, Australia.

His arrival in Australia was greeted with great enthusiasm, but nothing astonished Chichester more than his welcome home. Beacons were lit along the coast of Devon, and as Sunday 28 May 1967 dawned, over half a million people arrived in Plymouth to salute him from the shore. On 2 July, after a spell in hospital, he sailed for London, and at Greenwich, a few days later, he was knighted by the Queen.

'It was heavily overcast. The wind was now gusting at around forty knots and the combers, thought not so steep were still frighteningly high, the wind streaming the spume from the crests like clouds of steam.' Chichester had admitted, before setting sail from Plymouth, that nothing terrified him more than the waters approaching Cape Horn

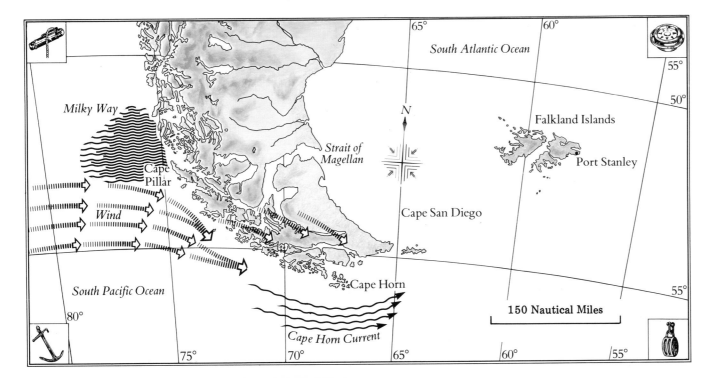

South Atlantic Ocean

65° 60° 55° 50°

Milky Way

N

Falkland Islands

Strait of Magellan

Cape Pillar

Wind

Port Stanley

Cape San Diego

South Pacific Ocean

150 Nautical Miles

Cape Horn

80°

Cape Horn Current

75° 70° 65° 60° 55°

Cape Horn

Gipsy Moth IV

BERNARD AND *JOSHUA*

Moitessier had left Plymouth in his steel-built Bermuda ketch on 22 August 1968 intending to sail round the world in the first single-handed race organised by the *Sunday Times* for the Golden Globe Trophy, and he had called her *Joshua* for a very good reason, as we shall learn.

On a squally June evening on 27 June 1898, approaching Long Island Sound, a lone mariner had heard a voice from the USS *Dexter* hail, '*Spray*, ahoy!' It was the end of a voyage lasting three years, which had given Joshua Slocum a place in maritime history as the first man ever to sail solo round the world.

Captain Slocum, who was born in Wilmot, Nova Scotia, in 1844, was a professional sailor and he had built *Spray* himself on the lines of an old oyster boat from the River Delaware. His life had already been laced with adventure, from fishing for a living in northern Alaska to quelling mutinies on board the clipper ship *Northern Light*, and he had not often stayed ashore.

Determined, at the age of fifty-four, to circumnavigate the world, Captain Slocum had left Boston in April 1895 and had sailed first to Gibraltar. But instead of continuing eastwards, he had then headed for the Straits of Magellan, where he was swamped by a tidal wave and then almost wrecked on the notorious 'Milky Way', north-west of Cape Horn. Renowned as the worst patch of water on earth, the only vessel

Joshua Slocum

Bernard Moitessier

known to have escaped from this maelstrom was at that time the famous HMS *Beagle*, but, undaunted, Slocum carried on. After a peaceful time in eastern Australia, and further adventures in the Indian Ocean, he sailed round the Cape of Good Hope, and back via the West Indies, having 'done nothing that an American sailor should be ashamed of', he barked at the New York press, on his arrival home.

Captain Slocum never explained about his methods of navigation, but stories are told of his old tin clock and the trailing 'log', almost bitten through by sharks. In 1909 *Spray* was completely refitted at the Herreshoff yard in Bristol, Rhode Island, as Slocum had the intention of sailing to the Orinoco. The great Nat Herreshoff waving him goodbye, was one of the last people to see the gallant captain alive. For Bernard Moitessier and many others Slocum has since become a legend, and christening his boat *Joshua* was very meaningful. 'There are just too many words,' said Moitessier one day, 'and finding the right ones is not an easy thing.'

He sailed down through the Atlantic, rounded the Cape of Good Hope and then, unlike his hero, he sped on eastwards, blasted by the Roaring Forties south of Tasmania and New Zealand, until he arrived off Cape Horn. Then, heading north again towards Europe after a record passage, he had second thoughts and catapulted a message to a passing ship which stated tersely: 'The Horn was rounded on February 5 . . . I am continuing non-stop towards the Pacific Islands, because I am happy at sea, and perhaps could also save my soul.'

On 21 June 1969, after a continuous 301 days on the ocean, eight months of which were spent in the Roaring Forties, he arrived without ceremony at Tahiti in French Polynesia. He had passed Australia twice, cir-

cumnavigated the globe one and a half times without stopping, and had accomplished one of the greatest feats of endurance ever recorded.

Several years later, soon after *Joshua* had met her end, driven ashore on a Mexican beach by a particularly violent storm, Bernard Moitessier, at an interview, recited this his favourite poem:

*. . . Je t'ai placé au milieu du monde afin que du puisses
mieux contempler ce que contient le monde.
Je ne t'ai fait ni celeste ni terrestre,
mortel ou immortel, afin que toi-meme,
librement, à la façon d'un bon peintre ou d'un
sculpture habile, tu achèves ta propre forme.*
  Pico della Mirandola (fourteenth century)

AUTHOR'S NOTE

On 28 May 1967, with my two brothers, I had flown over *Gipsy Moth IV* as she headed for Plymouth, in an ancient Auster flying machine (seen in the photograph on page 60) we then happened to own.

Surprisingly, and quite by coincidence, I also chanced to be visiting Tahiti in the same month that Bernard Moitessier arrived from his own epic journey round the world.

Once I had met an amazing fellow who had ridden on a bicycle the whole way from Punta Arenas in Chile to Anchorage in Alaska without it ever being acknowledged, and believing that Bernard's exploit had not been noticed either I put to him the question that he later had to answer frequently, often with the same reply: 'Why did you pull out of the *Sunday Times* race when you had such an excellent chance of winning?'

'Because', the Robinson Crusoe figure replied, 'I enjoy the solitude and racing for such records is an insult to the sea.'

Joshua arrives off the Polynesian Islands, watched curiously from a variety of native sailing craft

Joshua

WORLD CRUISING

SUNBEAM

The Gilbertian philosophy which insisted on adhesion to the desk and abstinence from the sea if a man's ambition were to be 'Ruler of the Queen's Navee', could hardly have been applied to Thomas Brassey, later Earl Brassey, Secretary to the Admiralty in 1884.

Brassey, who was born at Stafford in 1836, was the son of a pioneer of the railroads and like the Vanderbilts in America had inherited a vast fortune. A lover of the sea for all eighty-two years of his strenuous life, he was not for the *dolce far niente*, but a competent all-weather sailor, and when he commissioned *Sunbeam* at the age of thirty-eight in 1874, he was already in possession of the first Master's Certificate ever issued to a yachtsman.

Sunbeam was a magnificent schooner of 576 tons displacement, and one of the earliest to be powered by an auxiliary steam engine. Capable of driving her along at an average 7 knots using 4 tons of coal per day, the engine, fuelled by the 80 tons of coal in her bunkers, gave her a range of over 3,000 nautical miles without sail. She was equally effective sailing, and with her funnel folded to the deck she was once timed at 15 knots in a squall while crossing the North Pacific.

Sunbeam was always kept immaculate and had such an aura about her that when she entered Cowes Roads, she looked as much in keeping it was said 'as an old salt would at a tea party on the Squadron lawn.' At first painted black, Brassey had later experimented by changing one side to white, which must have been very confusing for the multitude of guests always being entertained on board. During her eminent career, subsequently painted all white, she was host to many

Admiral Lord Brassey

of the great personalities of her time including Mr Gladstone, the British Prime Minister, and the Poet Laureate, Alfred Tennyson. On the eve of the declaration of World War I Brassey entertained the German Admiral Von Tirpitz to a drink in the saloon, and wherever she went she was the watering hole for ambassadors, consuls, envoys and high commissioners throughout the world.

In 1860 Brassey married Annie, the only daughter of Mr John Allnut of Clapham, and it was she who was most responsible for his success. A constant companion in his travels, she contributed greatly to making him famous, and her book *The Voyage of the Sunbeam*, which has been republished many times, was translated into several languages and read throughout the world. In her book about their extraordinary forty-six-week circumnavigation of the world in 1876–7, written each morning sitting up in bed in their cabin, Annie Brassey describes the following scene off the coast of Tierra del Fuego in South America, which I have abbreviated:

Thursday, September 28th – A fine bright morning, the order to stop firing was given at noon and we ceased steaming shortly afterwards. There had evidently been a gale during the past few days, for the swell was tremendous. I was lying down below when Mabelle rushed into the cabin, saying, 'Papa says you are to come on deck at once, to see the ship on fire!' I rushed up quickly, hardly knowing whether she referred to our own or some other vessel, and on reaching the deck I found everybody looking at a large barque, under full sail, flying the red union-jack upside down. We were near enough to make out her name as the *Monkshaven of Whitby*. Her cargo, which apparently consisted of coal for smelting purposes, was a very dangerous one, and we had been told at Buenos Aires that, of every three ships carrying this cargo round to Valparaiso or Callao, one catches fire.

. . . It was perfectly evident that it would be impossible to save the ship, and some of the crew were accordingly at once brought aboard the *Sunbeam* in our boat, which was then sent back to assist in removing the remainder, a portion who came in their own boat. The poor fellows were almost wild with joy at getting alongside another ship.

. . . The poor little dinghy belonging to the *Monkshaven* had been cast away as soon as the men had disembarked, and there was something melancholy in seeing her slowly drift away to leeward. *Monkshaven* was now hove-to. The sky was dark and glowering,

Into the sunset

It's North you may run to the rime-ringed sun
    Or South to the blind Horn's hate;
Or East all the way into Mississippi Bay,
    Or West to the Golden Gate –
Where the blindest bluffs hold good dear lass,
    And the wildest tales are true,
And the men bulk big on the old trail, our own trail,
    the out trail,
And life runs large on the Long Trail – the trail that is always new.

O the blazing tropic night, when the wake's a welt of light
    That holds the hot sky tame,
And the steady fore-foot snores through the planet-powdered floors
    Where the sacred whale flukes in flame!
Her plates are flaked by the sun, dear lass,
    And her ropes are taut with the dew,
For we are booming down the old trail, our own trail, the out trail,
We're sagging south on the Long Trail – the trail that is always new.

Rudyard Kipling

the scene red and lurid in its grandeur. Not a breath of wind was stirring. Everything portended a gale. As we lay slowly rolling from side to side, both ship and boat were sometimes plainly visible, and then again both would disappear, for what seemed an age, in the deep trough of the South Atlantic rollers.

Tim Thompson's painting of the scene captures much of the drama that Annie Brassey described. *Sunbeam*'s other achievements are too numerous to relate, but in the great transatlantic race of 1905, she showed off her enduring qualities by finishing sixth. By the end of fifty-five years' cruising, latterly in the hands of the ship owner Lord Runciman, she had covered the astonishing distance of almost 600,000 miles.

Sunbeam rescues the crew of the *Monkshaven* off Tierra del Fuego

Monkshaven   *Sunbeam*

CREOLE – NEW WINE IN OLD BOTTLES

Some sailing yachts, usually the great survivors, stir such emotion in the hearts of men that they are talked about with a respect seldom given fellow mortals. *America, Reliance, Atlantic* and *Britannia* were all such vessels, but for us *Endeavour, Shamrock* and *Creole* may hold more magic, for they are still, after over half a century, very much alive.

To many, *Creole*, built in 1927, is still the most powerful-looking schooner afloat. Such is her charisma, that her ebony-black hull once recognised will instantly draw only one comment, a hissed '*Creole!*' Some will remember her at Dartmouth, filling the narrow estuary, her masts seemingly as high as the rising hills, or others at Cannes, bedecked in awnings with smart launches plying to and fro, or forging through the Straits of Gibraltar waited on by helicopters – photographers perhaps, or could it be the mail? Has she always been so magnificent we ask ourselves. Surprisingly, the answer is no.

Such immense yachts take a lot of handling, and when Alexander Cochran, who had previously commissioned *Westward*, took possession of her from the famous builders Camper & Nicholsons, he insisted on the carpenters lopping 15ft (4.5m) off each of her superb spruce masts. Already a very sick man, it was

Creole

said that at her launching the yard foreman had so doctored the bottle that it had to break, however weak the throw. But it also broke Cochran who, ordering the masts to be unstepped again, almost ruined the yacht by having yet another 15ft (4.5m) severed from her bleeding limbs. Cochran died soon afterwards and the 699 ton yacht, which he had at first called *Vira*, was bought by Major E. W. Pope and renamed *Creole*. Although his tastes had been modest, Cochran had insisted that she should be panelled in the finest veneers, and the yacht flinched once more when Pope, who probably knew no better, had all the beautiful cedar and sycamore painted over. Much to Camper & Nicholson's dismay he continued with her cut-down rig and, using her mainly for crossing from Southampton to the Royal Yacht Squadron at Cowes, he earned her the rather unglamorous nickname of 'Pope's Ferry'.

When Sir Connop Guthrie purchased her, already it seemed that *Creole* was going the same way as most other large schooners, changing hands frequently and each time being altered, seldom for the better. But to Charles Nicholson's delight, Guthrie instead decided to remast her and to reinstate her original sail plan. Guthrie sailed far and wide with *Creole*, using her appropriately as the comfortable cruising yacht for which she had been designed. But after many years of indulgence, war intervened and she was taken over by the Admiralty who, changing her name yet again to *Magic Circle*, gutted her and filled her with depolarising equipment so that she could track down magnetic mines. Because of certain technical advances, however, *Creole* was thankfully not called upon, and once the war was over she was handed back to her owners, mysteriously minus her masts. Some said that they had been destroyed in an air raid, but those who knew where she had been based understood the Scottish winters better.

Because Sir Connop had meanwhile died, his family now offered the yacht, *Creole* once more, back to Camper & Nicholsons at Gosport, who later sold her to the Danes as a training ship for very little money. When she broke a mast crossing the Atlantic, she came to the attention of one Stavros Niarchos, who soon bought her and had her re-engined and fitted out to almost her original design by the Imperial Shipping Company in Germany. For a time she then became the envy of the world.

Niarchos lavished every luxury on *Creole*, decorating her main saloon with murals by Salvador Dali, and filling a specially air-conditioned gallery with Cézannes, Renoirs, van Goghs, and works by Degas and Toulouse-Lautrec to name but a few. *Creole*, then the largest sailing ship in private hands, was often

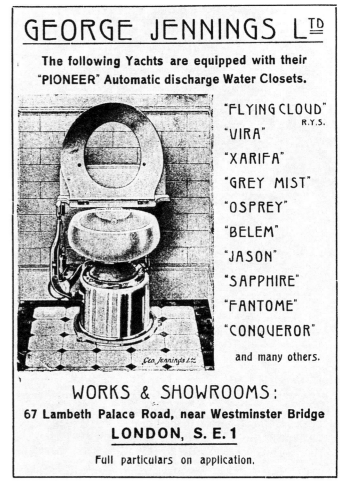
helmed by Niarchos, who would sometimes take her racing with her company of thirty-two. But above all he enjoyed entertaining, and *Creole* soon became a watering-hole for some of the best-known aristocrats around. Niarchos loved his *Creole*, and for many years spent half his time on board, but towards the end of the 1970s other distractions had intervened and poor *Creole* lay neglected in Piraeus, manned only by a skeleton crew.

If restoring venerable yachts to their former glory is beyond the reach of all but a few, the cost of restoring *Creole* was out of the question – except for one admirer, blessed with the family name of Gucci. At yards from Italy to Majorca, renowned for the best joinery work in Europe, her three proud masts have marked her convalescence, and now with ribs renewed in her tired frame, she is back to her old self again. New wine in an old bottle maybe, but perhaps it is not always so unlucky to change a ship's name.

Creole on trials off the Isle of Wight

Creole

A VANISHING BREED

The classic cruising yachts of the pre-war years have diminished in number far too quickly and are now, particularly in America, sought after like gold dust. Classic yacht regattas, held principally in the Mediterranean and at Newport, Rhode Island, are nostalgic occasions, not the least for owners of those yachts which have now vanished from the scene.

Panda, launched at the Northam yard of Camper & Nicholsons in 1938, at 200 tons, was the last of the grand British cruising yachts to be completed before World War II. Built of steel with high teak bulwarks, she gave an immediate impression of security, although her massive spruce mainmast made her a little tender in a blow. Her two diesels, which were similar to London bus engines, drove her at nearly nine knots under power, and in spite of her twin screws, which were unusual at the time, *Panda* could log fourteen knots when sailing off the wind.

After the war *Panda* was purchased by the French Government as an imperial yacht for the puppet Emperor Bao-Dai, ruler of Annam in French Indo-China, and her accommodation was altered to create a huge emporial cabin. By 1954, however, Bao-Dai was a political refugee living in Cannes, and the yacht remained unused and virtually unsaleable due to her lack of accommodation until purchased by a young twenty-three-year-old American, Sterling Hamill, who wanted to sail her round the world. After extensive cruising she was completely refitted, and with a crew of ten she was sailed to the Caribbean to become a charter yacht under different ownership. In 1985, while at anchor off Fort de France, Martinique, *Panda* mysteriously caught fire and sank in shallow water. Her owners refloated her, but the long tow necessary to a suitable boat yard proved prohibitively expensive, and her present whereabouts remain unknown.

Only the lighthouse on the Needles never changes, a memorial to a vanishing breed and the dream yachts of the past.

Panda off the Needles, Isle of Wight

68

The Needles Lighthouse

Panda

GUN-RUNNERS OR GIN PALACES?

Looking down on Monte Carlo and watching *Atlantis*, all 380ft (116m) of her, taking up her moorings is still an awe-inspiring sight. She looks like a liner, a great white whale of a ship, and as she swings it seems as if she'll push half the water, or as one person put it, her displacement of 'more than one million magnums of champagne', over the harbour wall. Nobody knows why Stavros Niarchos built such a goliath, for in 1974 he already owned *Mercury*, the first fifty-knot gasturbine yacht, and the stunningly beautiful schooner *Creole*. Was it to cruise the world, or just to entertain? Was it to hang the Andy Warhols in the bar, two giant paintings of Elvis Presley, or to outdo *Christina*, then the most famous motor yacht of all?

Aristotle Socrates Onassis or Ari to his friends, loved beautiful women, but nothing in life was more special to him than the lovely *Christina*, which, on first appearing on the scene in 1954, was the most luxurious yacht afloat, and the undisputed 'belle of the Monte Carlo ball'. Parties were numerous, the guest lists impeccable, and the caviare mountainous, usually washed down with plenty of ouzo. Onassis even had his bread flown in each day specially from Paris, but so

Plans showing the layout of the first Katalina, *now* Klementine

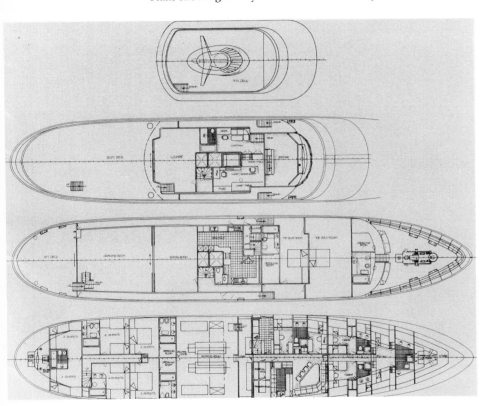

it should be, when the ship's complement might include Sir Winston and Lady Churchill, Maria Callas or Greta Garbo. *Christina* had a hydraulically operated swimming pool, which converted to a dance floor, and on deck a primrose-yellow amphibian for flying his friends ashore. But she had nothing on some of the post-war mega-yachts to follow.

In 1980 Adnan Kashoggi, the noted Saudi Arabian businessman, built *Nabila*, the most spectacular yacht yet seen. Since sold and renamed *Trump Princess* it is now estimated that her running costs are well in excess of $M3.5 per year. *Nabila* can carry fifty-six crew, including five chefs, and twenty-two guests in eleven cabins. She has three lifts and a hospital with an operating theatre suitable for open heart surgery. Her interior is lavishly decorated with exquisite marble and the gold plating alone is worth more than $M2. But although she would now cost no less than $M70 to build, this huge figure has already been eclipsed by others.

Many of these yachts have just become part of the furniture. How would Cannes or Juan les Pins look without them, we ask; like New York without Manhattan or London without St Paul's? But some of the more adventurous yachts are seldom to be seen – none more dashing than the discreet *Katalina*s.

The first *Katalina* had been launched from the Amels yard in Holland in 1982. She was a splendid vessel of just over 48m (157ft), with a permanent crew of eleven, including a captain, mate, engineer, purser, two stewards, two cooks, a second engineer and two deckhands, and she cruised at a good twelve knots. Her proving voyage was to Antigua in the West Indies, and then she did a round trip to Antibes in the South of France. But her owner's eyes were on the far horizons, not on the playgrounds of the Mediterranean or the Caribbean, and in April 1984 she set out through the Panama Canal to the Galapagos and Marquesas Islands and then on to Polynesia in the South Pacific. Tahiti welcomed *Katalina*, for such yachts are few and far between, and as she continued her cruise to Samoa, Tonga and Fiji, some may have thought back a hundred years to the famous voyage of the *Sunbeam*.

Katalina's owner had meanwhile developed a passion for spearfishing, and to supplement the rations, he and her captain would dive on the coral reefs bringing back a harvest of every kind of fish. Off the Solomon Islands they were to dive amongst over a hundred sharks, feeding in a frenzy, and later on a reef south of Indonesia, they had to retreat from a squadron of deadly poisonous sea snakes, and go back to eating biscuits! It was cruising in the great traditions of the oceans, exploring this time the underwater world, sometimes, no doubt, where man had never been.

In 1987 the second *Katalina* was launched. This time over 65m (213ft) long, she carries a crew of twenty. She is a superb yacht, with all the latest communication equipment and navigational aids, as well as a helicopter flight deck and a two-man decompression chamber, for divers' safety (Oil sketch for a larger painting of *Katalina II*)

In September 1985 *Katalina* had left the Marshall Islands for Singapore, and one of her worst moments was later in the Maldives where she hit a propeller on a knob of coral and had to limp many hundreds of miles to achieve some kind of repair. It was while she was at Cochin in India that all her undeclared cash was sequestered plus 160 crates of beer.

When she returned to Palma, Majorca in April 1986, having entertained the King and Queen of Jordan in Aqaba and been falsely accused in Rhodes of gunrunning on the way, she had, in twenty-six months, covered no less than eighty-four thousand nautical miles around the globe. Gun runner or Gin Palace, *Katalina*, since renamed *Klementine*, is a very special yacht indeed.

The first Katalina *off the Pitons, Virgin Islands*

M.Y. Katalina

12 METRE
RACING

GRETEL THE GREAT

The outbreak of World War II had put paid to the 'Big Class' for once and for all, or so it seemed, and no longer were the magnificent Js or schooners to be seen thrashing to windward with vast crews packed like sardines along the weather rail. For apart from economic reasons there was now much more interest in ocean racing and many of the super yachts had proved far too frail. In many ways it was the designers themselves who were to blame. The lessons learned from the mighty *Reliance* it was apparent had not struck home, and they were still drawing such out and out racing machines that, being suitable for no other purpose, nobody wanted to own them.

As far back as 1907 some class boat enthusiast had thought up the 12 Metre, and in 1922 John Payne had ordered, at a cost of £4,500, his first Twelve, the famous *Vanity*, from Fife. Built to what was known as the second International Rule, she was 65ft (20m) overall and carried 2,100sq ft (195sq m) of sail. In 1928 T. O. M. Sopwith had asked Charles Nicholson to design the successful 12 Metre *Mouette*, which, being subsequently sold to America, created an immediate interest there. The International Yacht Racing Union in order to encourage the new class amended the rules again in 1934 and, as a result, in the last British regatta season before the war there were eight 12 Metres, joined by Mike Vanderbilt's remarkable winning yacht *Vim*.

Vim had been designed by Olin Stephens and when in 1958, long after hostilities were over, Hugh Goodson put together an America's Cup challenge with the British 12 Metre *Sceptre*, Stephens was already acknowledged as the best designer of 'the finest class of yachts in the world'. Following the match, which Stephens's *Columbia* won with a clean sweep, and

while the Royal Thames Yacht Club were trying their damnedest to put another attempt together, out of the wide blue southern hemisphere came a challenge from the Australian, Frank Packer, through the Royal Sydney Yacht Squadron which, much to the annoyance of the British, the New York Yacht Club accepted.

Gretel, designed by Alan Payne, was launched on 28 February 1962 at a colourful ceremony in Sydney watched over by the veteran *Vim*, who this time, like *Mouette* in America before her, had spread the disease to Australia. America's Cup fever was catching on, and *Gretel* was their first home-built 12 Metre ever. Alan Payne had done an excellent job and, although not particularly innovative, *Gretel* had fine lines and he had acquired for her the latest aerodynamically shaped rod rigging. Although the New York Yacht Club had insisted that she should be designed and built in Australia, Payne had tank tested thirty different models, based on the chartered *Vim*, at the Stevens Institute of Technology, and her eighty sails were cut from American Dacron, being the only decent material available. Just over 69ft (21m) in overall length, she had a full beam amidships, giving her stability and power in any seaway which was to prove greatly to her advantage later.

On 15 September, when the two combatants met for the first race off Newport, the morale of the Australian supporters was raised by the forecast of eighteen-knot winds. *Gretel* seemed able to cope with most conditions, but she particularly liked heavy weather, which Emil 'Bus' Mosbacher, at the helm of the American yacht *Weatherly*, it was rumoured, did not. Just before the start 'Jock' Sturrock at *Gretel*'s helm managed to break away from the wily Mosbacher and set Australian hearts pounding by crossing the line eight seconds in the lead. It was not to last, for initially a navigational error (electronic aids were being used for the first time), and then a broken backstay gave *Weatherly* the race by almost four minutes.

On board *Gretel*, changing sails

In the second race *Gretel* was again first over the line, but this time she was out for blood. On the first windward leg the yachts engaged in one of the most exciting duels ever seen, and Mosbacher, if he had not already sensed it, now realised that he was up against an exceptional 12 Metre. As *Gretel* turned the final mark, Sturrock ran up a huge white spinnaker and, with her crew whooping with excitement, she shot down the waves like a giant surfboard, flew past *Weatherly* in a welter of spray, and surged over the finishing line a triumphant forty-seven seconds ahead.

The secret weapon had been revealed. Payne had designed the yacht with such a long, flat run that she would almost sit up on the waves and plane, touching fifteen knots on the crests.

The third race, held in changeable weather, was won by Mosbacher, who was a master in light winds. Payne, realising before the contest that smart sail handling could win the day, had linked up two 'coffee-grinder' winches so that the strength of four men could be harnessed to one sheet. It almost came off. The remaining races were both thrillers, and although *Weatherly* was the victor, they provided some of the best crew work and tightest finishes in the cup's history.

After it was all over *Gretel* was herself tank tested, and the director of the Stevens Institute agreed that the Aussie yacht, at their first attempt, was the faster boat. No wonder that the folks back home named her '*Gretel* the great'.

Like a giant surfboard, *Gretel* shoots down the waves to overtake *Weatherly* and win the second race.

Gretel's coffee-grinders

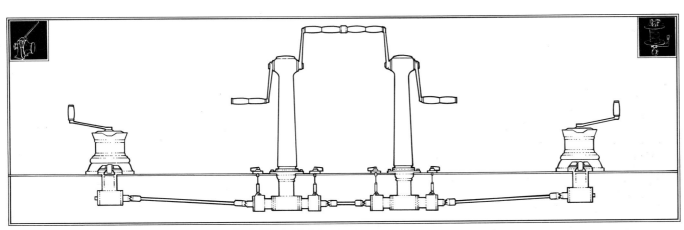

Gretel

THE MAGIC KEEL

In 1983 the Australians were back at Newport for their seventh attempt to win the America's Cup. Starting with the defeat of *Gretel* in 1962, and with the exception of the British challenger *Sovereign* in 1964, it had been a sustained and relentless attack with *Dame Pattie* losing in 1967, *Gretel II* losing in 1970, *Southern Cross* losing in 1974, and *Australia* being defeated in both 1977 and in 1980. The defences were more impregnable than ever, it seemed, for out of a total of twenty-four races the Australians had to date won only three. But there were two fighters who would not lay down their arms, men so battle worn that they were prepared to carry on at any cost, only that one of them, Ben Lexcen, had a much more subtle plan.

Lexcen had been working with Alan Bond for twelve years to lift the cup to Western Australia, and they both appreciated the great opportunities which would then be presented. Lexcen's own story had something of the ring of 'rags-to-riches' about it too, but money did not bother him, he just liked to be creative, and at that he was a genius.

For Lexcen his first challenger the 'stone banana', as some Americans dubbed Bond's 'Yanchep yellow' *Southern Cross*, was somewhat of a disaster. Jim Hardy, her helmsman was later reported as saying, 'I slept like a baby – for after the first race, I woke up every two hours and cried.' It ranked Lexcen to let down Bondy so badly, and so he took off from Australia to live for a time in Cowes. Bond was having nothing of it and flew to England to fetch Ben Lexcen home. Taking him under his wing, he encouraged Lexcen about his outstanding abilities, and together they swore never to rest until they brought the cup back to Perth.

In 1983 *Australia II*'s victory over the American yacht *Liberty* was attributed largely to her innovative winged keel. Although not an original concept, the idea had been perfected directly by the introduction of new computer modelling techniques

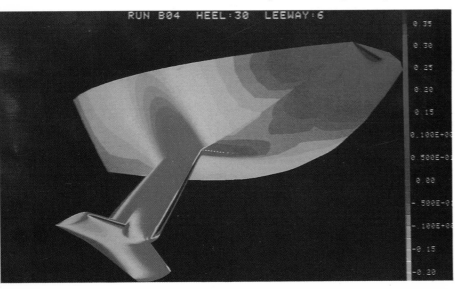

Ben Lexcen had been playing with the idea of a winged keel as far back as the early sixties, and after *Australia*'s defeat in 1980, he began to put into effect his master plan. *Australia* on that occasion had been fitted with a 'bendy' mast, copied at the last moment from the British contender *Lionheart*, and because the Americans were too late to make one for themselves Bondy had it floodlit at night. Lexcen had been interested to see *Freedom*'s skipper Dennis Conner apparently rattled by this, and it appealed to both him and his boss to drive the message home. 'No holds barred!' Whether the winged keel was going to be a breakthrough or purely a psychological 'hype' really did not matter. Lexcen had been encouraged by Peter van Oossanen at the Netherlands Ship Model Basin, where German U-boats had been designed during the occupation, to analyse his ideas in any case. So he first tested a conventional Twelve and then added the appendages until the computers began to crackle.

The upside-down keel fitted to 'Flying Fifteens' had been the brainchild of the British designer Uffa Fox, and it was this principle that had gripped Lexcen's imagination. But suddenly it was all for real. It actually worked, and Bond arrived from Australia with John Bertrand, his skipper, to see it.

Australia II was born in an old tin shed at Cove Haven, just off the Perth–Fremantle highway. So great was the secrecy surrounding her that even Bondy one day could not get in. Then they wrapped her up like a parcel, shipped her off to Newport, and got the tongues of the world's press wagging. The Americans had their spies out even before the ship had docked. The Aussies were concealing something big they surmised, for it simply was not like them to 'hide behind a skirt!'

There then followed the most determined attempt that yachting had ever known to ban a competitor, and as *Australia II* began to carve her way through the elimination series the protests hotted up. First came allegations from the New York Yacht Club that the keel made her unfairly rated, then that the Australian boat had been designed in Holland in total disregard for the rules. 'This is not sport. It's war!' claimed Bond.

The final assault was launched on 26 September 1983. The score, at three wins each, left all to play for, and as *Australia II* passed Conner's *Liberty* near the very last mark on the course, the whole of Australia ground to a standstill. The Americans had been defeated not only by great skill, but as Lexcen would have it, at last by the faster boat. 'Keep 'em guessing', he had once exhorted Bond, but such was Bondy's exuberance that he unveiled the magic keel – in a moment he lived to regret, for by 1987 all the America's Cup yachts had copied it.

BEN LEXCEN

Bob Miller's family had moved from the wilderness of the Australian bush to the East Coast in 1943, when he was only seven. Seeing the deep blue waters of the Pacific had guided the hand of destiny, and within a short time he was making model boats.

After a brief spell at school he was turned down for his first job in a boat yard and went to work on the railways. However, he found time to crew a leaking skiff *Adele*, and at Lake Macquarie Yacht Club, because of all his theorising, quickly earned the name of 'The Professor'. He built his own 23ft (7m) boat when only just sixteen, and later was responsible for two grossly overcanvased 18 footers (5.5m) which were to influence the future of open-boat sailing in Australia.

Bob then teamed up with a fellow enthusiast Craig Whitworth to start a sailmaking business and by 1971 their turnover had reached $300,000. He had been dreaming of designing an America's Cup challenger since he was in his twenties, and in 1965 he abandoned his business to concentrate on drawing boats. Success came quickly with *Mercedes III* which, after the Admiral's Cup of 1967, was acknowledged as the world's leading ocean-racing yacht.

He met Alan Bond in 1969, when Bond came to inspect his Miller-designed *Apollo*. From her, while they were both sailing in America, Bond spied his first 12 Metre. 'What's the America's Cup?' Bondy asked Miller. Then, listening to his reply, he barked: 'Right, you design me one of those 12 Metres and we'll come back here and win their bloody Cup'.

(Ever since leaving Craig Whitworth, Bob Miller had been thinking about a new professional name. In 1974 he announced that he was in future to be called Ben Lexcen.) Very sadly, at the age of only 52, Ben died in April, 1988.

The moment of truth

Australia II   *Liberty*

Crusader II   *Crusader I*

STARS AND SUPERSTARS

The 1987 America's Cup winner *Stars & Stripes* was a superstar, right from the time she came off the drawing board. She was a genuine beauty of a yacht, not flashy or even full of new ideas, but just designed with tremendous care, and at vast expense, to make the best of Western Australian conditions and to keep the 'Doctor', the wicked Fremantle wind, firmly in his place.

Not long after Dennis Conner had suffered his humiliating defeat with *Liberty* in 1983, he received a tentative invitation from the New York Yacht Club to get things together again, but when attempts to make arrangements failed, he decided to win the Cup back by himself. It was a brave decision by a man of considerable, almost obsessive, determination. He had set about finding sponsors immediately, and backed subsequently by such hefty 'godfathers' as Meryll Lynch and Ford, he collected many millions of dollars and probably the fattest purse of the lot. Then, aided by NASA and by the most powerful computers in the world, he built himself first three and then a fourth superb gunsmoke-blue yacht.

For a time it looked as if he was beaten, but as the elimination series between the fourteen challengers progressed and the winds strengthened, eventually the gallant *Magic Kiwi* and finally the laughing *Kookaburra* (named after an exuberant Australian bird), coughed, spluttered, and gave up.

America's Cup winners are no longer stars but superstars, and they sail better now on molten gold, than on all the salt water we've got.

◀ The British *Crusaders*, seen turning up off Fremantle, were never given superstar status and were brought on stage too late

Dennis Conner ducks *Stars & Stripes* under *Kookaburra*'s stern, ▶ the most powerful move in the finals of the 1987 series

Kookaburra   Stars & Stripes

DEVELOPMENT OF THE YACHT

HULL DESIGN

The evolution of the sailing hull is a fascinating, if not somewhat obscure, story.

About 4,500 years ago, probably in some Middle Eastern creek, and later, on a shelving beach in the islands of the Pacific maybe, two distinct types of hull were born, each for different reasons. The single-hulled load-carrying Middle Eastern boat, in order to maintain stability in the wind, was built with a low centre of gravity and eventually a keel, but the Pacific boat, which had to skim the coral and be launched from sand, was built with an extra hull or outrigger, which kept it upright and in certain conditions gave it tremendous speed. Each type of boat, until quite recently, was kept separated by history, the concept of the single or monohulled vessel spreading westwards through the Mediterranean, Europe, Africa and the Americas, and eastwards to the China Seas, and the concept of the multihull spreading south to the Australias and west to islands of Indonesia.

Although the multihull has since been developed to travel at twice the speed of the wind, the monohull, not through culture or aesthetics but because of its intrinsic power and rigidity, has been given the greater attention, and its growing combination of design features has become virtually inexhaustible.

In Europe it was perhaps only natural that sailing should first have been developed by the Dutch. The first Dutch yachts were fitted with leeboards which rotated on a pivot so that, depending on the tack or the yacht's course in relation to the wind direction, the angle of attack could be suitably adjusted and the yacht steered in the most efficient way. The yacht *Mary* sailed to England so equipped, and hull designs remained largely unaltered for the best part of a further two hundred years.

After the formation of the Cumberland Fleet in 1775, British designers, encouraged by the new national sport of yacht racing, began to be slightly more imaginative, and by the close of the century some attempts had been made to get away from the bluff bow and full beam inherited from Holland. Up to that time these 'cod's head and mackerel tailed' vessels had been built unnecessarily solid, and the heavy-weight

lifting of ballast to the windward side each time they were tacked just added to the difficulties of sailing them. The building of such famous cutters as the *Arrow* and the *Alarm* was somewhat better conceived, but it was not until the years following the surprise attack by the yacht *America* in 1851 that the old habits were finally broken, and the lines for an ideal craft properly investigated.

But however hard they tried, the British were not about to catch up. Developed on her great stretches of inland water the American scows or skimming dishes were also by now gaining a marked ascendancy over their European rivals, and in light conditions these shoal-draught yachts with retractable centreboards soon became almost unbeatable. Indeed by 1880 it was only amongst the ocean-going schooners, some of which had also been fitted with centreboards – an idea patented in 1811 by the Swain brothers of New Jersey – that heavy displacement hulls were to be found anywhere on the American continent.

In Victorian England the conditions which favoured the Americans were then almost unknown. Accustomed mainly to competing at sea, in the Firth of Clyde, the

Yachts racing in the Solent

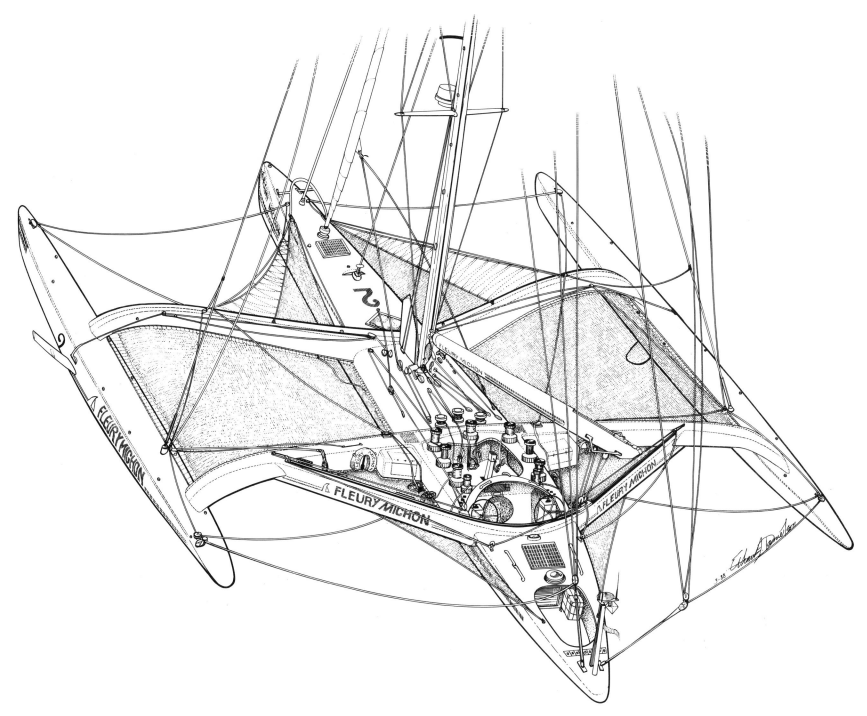

Solent or Torbay, vessels were constantly reduced in width and increased in length and depth, some becoming six times longer than they were in beam. Throughout the next few years this tendency increased, so that by 1886, aggravated by one poor rating rule after another, yachts had become so deep and narrow that they had been labelled 'planks on edge'. The wreck of the yacht *Oona* at this time off the Irish coast, when her keel dropped off and all hands including her designer were lost, brought some to their senses, but it was no better in America where the centreboard schooner *Mohawk* had capsized, drowning several on board including some ladies. The current America's Cup ruling, forcing British yachts to first sail the Atlantic, also seemed to many increasingly unfair, and the debate as to the best type, 'skimming dish' or 'plank on edge', continued to hot up.

Needless to say such a 'heady' atmosphere was breath to the designers, and it was in this environment that many famous names like George Watson and William Fife in Great Britain, and Nat Herreshoff and Edward Burgess in America soon hit the limelight. 'Yacht architecture is a compound of three diverse elements', stated one correspondent. 'Fad and craze with an occasional degree of economy, the quirks of mathematical measurement rules, and the genuine desire to produce the ideal yacht.'

After such a period of contradiction, surprisingly there followed the launching of some of the most beautiful and extravagant yachts ever built, their designs so impressive that in 1893 *Satanita*, the largest of England's new racing cutters, carried so much canvas that she was sometimes unmanageable. During 1901, in America Thomas Lawson had commissioned a brute of a yacht with long overhangs called *Independence*, which was so unseaworthy that she had to be scrapped almost as soon as she sailed, and *Reliance*, the America's Cup defender of 1903, had then followed her lines but with such a massive rig that she more resembled a giant butterfly. At an international conference held in London in 1906 and attended by most European seafaring nations, rules were drawn up which, by regularising design, in effect underwrote the new concept of class racing. The suggested rating system, which has since only been twice modified, still governs the construction of all 12 Metres today.

In America, where they raced by the Universal Rule first introduced by Nat Herreshoff, no genuine attempt was made to put their house in order until 1925, when the North American Yacht Racing Union was formed. Meanwhile yachts on both sides of the Atlantic were edging closer in design, but only by unwritten compromise. On one side of the ocean the International Rule was hardly international, and on the other side the Universal Rule was by no means universal; it seemed a crazy situation. In 1927, however, while keeping to their traditional M, P, Q and R classes, the Americans decided to accept the International Yacht Racing Union classes of 6, 8, 10 and 12 Metres, and this was the first determined step to standardise competition.

During the years between the two world wars, although the 'Big Class' regattas under handicap continued to produce some of the most spectacular yachting ever seen in England, the new Bermudian rig was already encouraging more One Design racing, while in the United States, Starling Burgess, who had spent World War I designing aircraft, now put his mind to creating yachts with high-performance hulls fashioned out of aluminium. The Americans seemed to be getting their own way again, and with the advent of the J class they once more turned the tables and reverted to the Universal Rule.

The only rule that is of any significance today, however, is the International Offshore Rule (IOR), first drafted in 1912, and now an amalgam of all that has been disputed in the past hundred or more years. It is a complex rule brimming with mathematical formulas, but in science although beauty may be acceptable measurement is sadly the only truth. The rule is for 'habitable' boats now taking part in most of the world's main yachting events, and skippers who can wave a valid IOR certificate at the organisers of a race either of level rating or one of corrected time can be assured that their yacht will be treated with the utmost impartiality. The class to which the rule does not

apply is the multihulls. If speed, seaworthiness and comfort are three measures of progress in monohull yacht design through the ages, then for multihulls there is only one: speed. In comparison to monohulls, which to the detriment of seaworthiness and comfort have constantly been shedding weight to gain speed, the recent increase in multihull performance has been little short of astonishing. The multihull has few weight problems, no ballast to contend with, no lead-filled keel, just a wide spread of struts and braces that somehow must keep it from breaking up or capsizing in a heavy sea. The multihull is the ideal vehicle for testing the latest advances in high-technology construction, but it does have two lasting problems, its shape in confined spaces and its poor performance when sailing into wind.

Multihulls have their own important place in the record books but they live separate lives to the monohulls except in the world of ocean racing. In order to compete with them, monohull construction has also gone through some profound changes, and the industry has had to adapt itself, perhaps too quickly, to new space-age materials and the techniques of computerisation. At times these innovative designs have been severely tested, never more so than during the Fastnet race of 1979, and perhaps we should stand back and ask ourselves sometimes are our present designers being really so imaginative, or are they, by sacrificing everything for speed, turning the full circle and creating racing yachts which are merely copies of those American scows, which were so successful at the very beginning of the twentieth century.

Nat Herreshoff

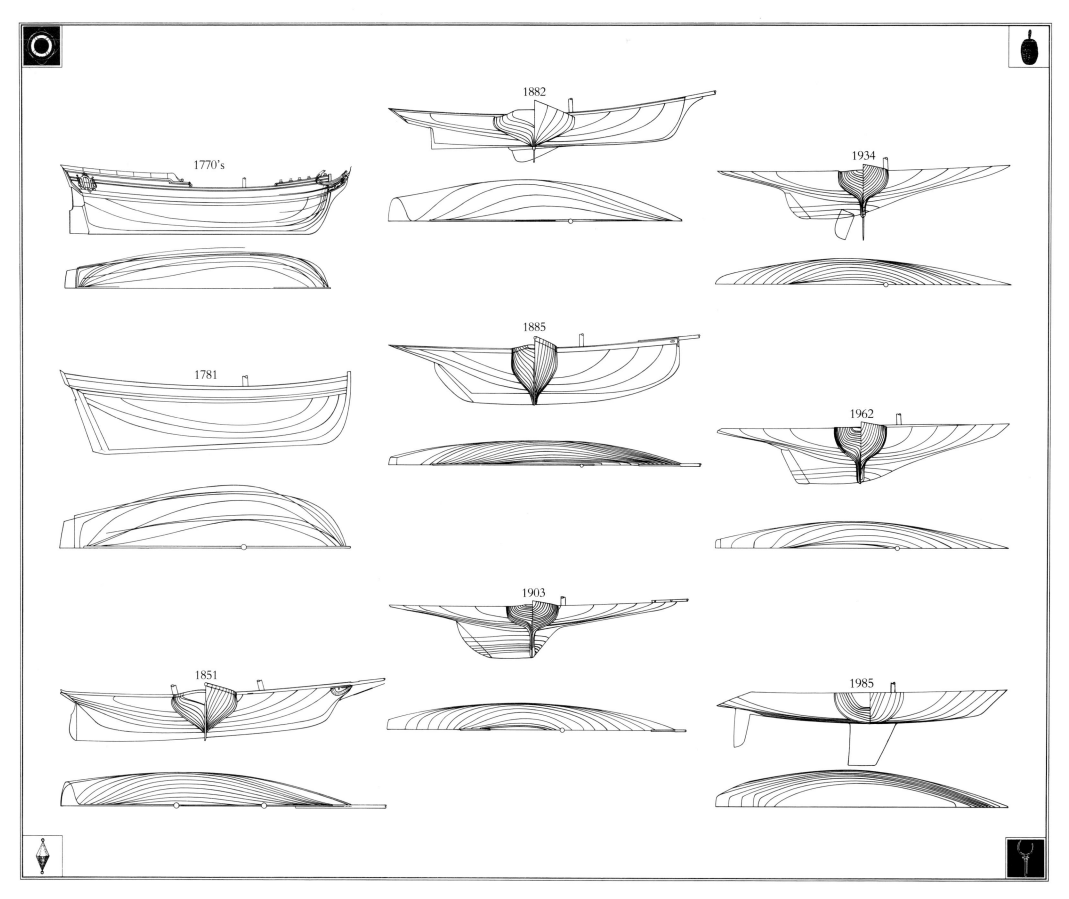

Hull shapes. Note the American scow of 1882 compared with the British 'plank on edge' of 1885 and the return to the scow type hull for the 1985 maxis

YACHT BUILDING

We have not exhausted the possibilities of form yet . . . when we do arrive at perfection of shape, we can set to then, and look for better materials.

George Watson, 1881

For countless centuries boats had been constructed almost exclusively of wood, and when George Watson, later to design *Britannia*, made this profound statement it looked as if the yacht-building industry was running out of ideas.

Successful yacht design is, to a large extent, the outcome of an artist's inspiration, but a designer will get nowhere if he does not have a detailed understanding of the materials he is working in. Somehow wood had always given designers that inner confidence, and a yacht's scantlings or stress requirements never seemed a problem. Designers were used to stems and sternposts fashioned in seasoned English oak, to the special qualities of east India teak, or Honduras mahogany, and to pitch-pine planking shipped only from the southern states of North America. With constraints of no greater consequence than the direction of the grain or the size of the tree trunk, yachts could be chalked out on the builder's floor and grow to more or less any desired proportion. But wood, despite its long-lasting nature, had one great disadvantage: in earlier designs of yachts it was nearly always extremely heavy.

One step forward was to fit steamed wood-strap frames to the inside of a hull once it had been planked, and this tended to reduce the weight somewhat, but in England by the middle of the nineteenth century wooden yachts were alternatively being framed in iron, the King's yacht *Britannia* being constructed this way in 1893. These composite designs came about largely as a result of the Industrial Revolution, but also because of the new lead keels which were now bolted on to the hull. They were renowned for their strength and longevity, but it was not until 1925 that Lloyd's Register took account of these changes, at the same time confining their longer-lasting certificate to vessels with brass or copper fastenings. Lloyd's, which is not part of the insurance market, had registered its first wooden yacht *Saunterer* (subsequently owned by Captain Titus Oates of Scott's ill-fated 1912 Antarctic Expedition) in the year 1900. Although registration has never been compulsory, a Lloyd's + 100 A1 certificate has always meant a great deal, particularly when selling a yacht, while other countries, including America, have their own similar, if not more onerous, sets of yacht-building regulations.

Before long, towards the end of the century, the composite hull was being replaced with some yachts totally built of iron. Also a very durable material, it proved itself to be almost as satisfactory as the all-steel construction which followed. Both iron and steel were obviously prone to rusting, but new coatings which evolved over a period of many years slowly helped control the problem. Today a few boats are being built in stainless steel.

In about the year 1890, the much lighter metal aluminium was used for the first time in yacht building, but it was little understood. Approximately half the weight of steel, it unfortunately corroded in salt water combining with some metals to cause electrolysis, as discovered to the cost of the American yacht *Defender* in 1895. But by 1930 many of these difficulties had been ironed out, and by using aluminium alloys and new welding techniques, or the clever combination of glue and riveting by 1980 it became the favoured material for racing boats, possessing exceptional strength and stiffness.

After World War I when metals and good timber were in short supply it was fortunate that new marine glues had been developed, which made it possible to veneer layer upon layer of thin, comparatively unseasoned, wood over a mould, and thereby construct a strong but even lighter hull. Although this method of cold moulding is still practised today, after World War II it was largely superseded by the introduction of glass-reinforced plastics (GRP). GRP or glass-fibre hull mouldings were first accepted by designers as short a time ago as the early 1950s, and within a few years had replaced most other materials for yachts up to 100ft (30m) in overall length. Although a few small builders, mostly for reasons of simplicity, had also some success with reinforced concrete or ferrocement, it tended again to be heavy, whilst glass fibre seemed to have everything and was easy to maintain.

But one quality (apart from later problems with water saturation or osmosis, now remedied by better curing procedures) was missing, namely rigidity. It was soon found necessary to include such additional supports in the structure of the hull that much of the weight advantage was lost. This has now been largely overcome by better design, the inclusion of a foam- or honeycomb-sandwiched core, the addition of advanced plastics and by the use of carbon fibre for certain fittings. Even this material was not man enough for the rigours of the 1979 Fastnet race, and as a result space-age titanium may also now form part of many new constructions.

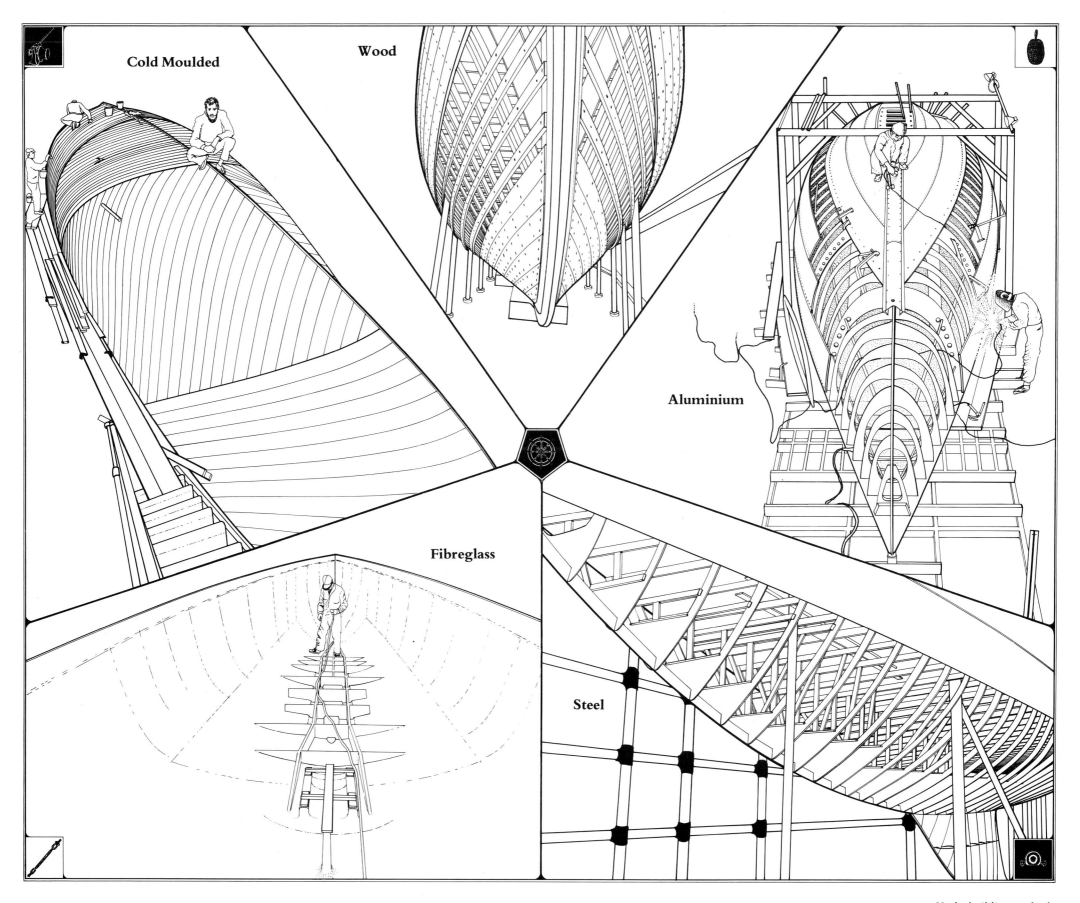

Cold Moulded

Wood

Aluminium

Fibreglass

Steel

Yacht-building methods

RIGS AND SAILMAKING

There is now little distinction between jibs and staysails except that if two headsails are carried the outermost is called the jib. Vessels carrying more than a single headsail were often fitted with a bowsprit and Falconer, in his *Marine Dictionary* of 1769, described such yachts as cutters. The Revenue cutters of the eighteenth century had been used principally to catch pirates and smugglers, but when the smugglers began gaining the ascendancy in their square-rigged luggers, the British Government responded by adding for the first time topsails to two additional masts.

At the time of the Restoration, sails had first been made of coarse French canvas. However, King Charles II, unmindful of the privy purse, was soon encouraging the more expensive use of Holland duck. It was not for many years that English flax was used, and it was only when the yacht *America* arrived in England in 1851 that any attempt was made to make another change. The British, whose baggy sails of loosely woven material had to be wetted constantly to hold the wind, were astonished by the board-like appearance of the *America*'s rig and, realising that the American machine-spun white cotton duck was a great deal better than their own, their orders were soon being sent to the United States instead.

A quite different rig to evolve during the 1820s in Europe was that of the ketch. Because the fishing fleets were having to go further afield for a catch, their boats had become larger and the old lug sails more difficult to manage. So instead they opted for boomless gaff mainsails with an additional small mast just forward of the rudder, calling the boat a ketch. It was a strong, simple rig that was easy to adjust, so for yachts it was a natural, as it was again some seventy years later when the mizzen was at times placed aft of the rudder and the yacht called a yawl instead.

The Bermudian rig was once again claimed to be an American baby, conceived in Bermuda as early as 1883 but not born in Massachusetts until 1914 while the British were at war. The high-aspect-ratio rig was a winner from the start, saving weight aloft by reducing the amount of running gear and spars, but since the thirties and the days of the tender 'J' boats, which were often unseaworthy in a decent blow, it has been considerably altered. As the mainsail has become shorter at the foot, power has been transferred to the headsails, while the staysails have been slowly disappearing, being less efficient than the modern genoas when the breeze is forward of the beam. Whereas the cutters of the nineteenth century pointed at fifty degrees, it is

84

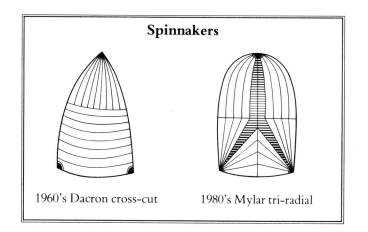

Spinnakers

1960's Dacron cross-cut   1980's Mylar tri-radial

claimed that with the latest rigs many yachts will soon be sailing at an unbelievable thirty-five degrees into the wind.

Sailcloth has meanwhile changed dramatically, with cotton giving way to rayon, (first used by Ranger in 1937) and the too elastic nylon, then to ICI Terylene, while Tergal was developed in France, and in 1958 to Dacron by Dupont in the United States. The small world of sailmakers, such as Ratsey & Lapthorn in Great Britain and Hood or North in America, were always looking for the breakthrough and cutting more advanced and stable shapes. By 1974 the America's Cup defender *Courageous* was using a Kevlar, an immensely strong material but bugged by Dacron stitching, while spinnakers were later made of Mylar, which seemed to split only along the seams. And so the quest continues; Kevlar/Mylar, Laminar or Hood's more recent Spectra. Perhaps we shall never find the perfect material or for that matter, like the world of fashion ever cut the perfect sail.

Old spinnaker compared with new type.

The first-known spinnaker, triangular in shape, was flown from the topmast of a yacht at Cowes in 1865 and quickly gained acceptance, although solely for running directly before the wind. Subsequently in the thirties a new 'parachute' spinnaker was developed for class racing, which could be sheeted to leeward of the forestay, and was used extensively by the Js. The British 'Annie Oakley' (as it seemed to be shot full of holes) and the American 'Mae West' (somewhat voluminous) spinnakers held the stage for several years, but after World War II balloon spinnakers, flown from lower down the mast, became more fashionable. Tri-radial, crosscut, floater, flanker, starcut and tri-star jumbo spinnakers are yet another dimension of the sailmaker's art. Now designed to suit every possible condition and sometimes hoisted to the masthead with a 'Big Boy' or 'Blooper' to fill the gap between the mainsail, they can drive a boat along not only when she's reaching but almost into wind.

Old jib compared to new jib.

Jibs were always made on various sizes. The no. 1 for example was the general working sail, the no. 2, smaller and heavier, was for fresher winds, and the 'storm' or 'spitfire' jib was essential for keeping the yacht head to sea in a gale. Jibs at first were triangular, made of American or Egyptian cotton, and cut diagonally with a wire luff, but *Endeavour*, the America's Cup challenger in 1934, experimented with a quadrilateral jib, in which the leech was cut short and the lower part carried down parallel to the luff, to give the sail two clews. Although the idea was copied by the American defender *Rainbow* and was used through until 1937, it was subsequently dropped and today, vertical cut, spider-cut, rocked-panelled and radial-corner jibs are almost triangular again, but with cleverly curved edges. By the time of the America's Cup of 1983 sailmaking had made considerable technical advances, and in 1987 the Australian defender *Kookaburra*, copying an old photographic technique first used by Harold Vanderbilt in 1930, had black strips attached to her sails so that their shape could be monitored, this time, by computer.

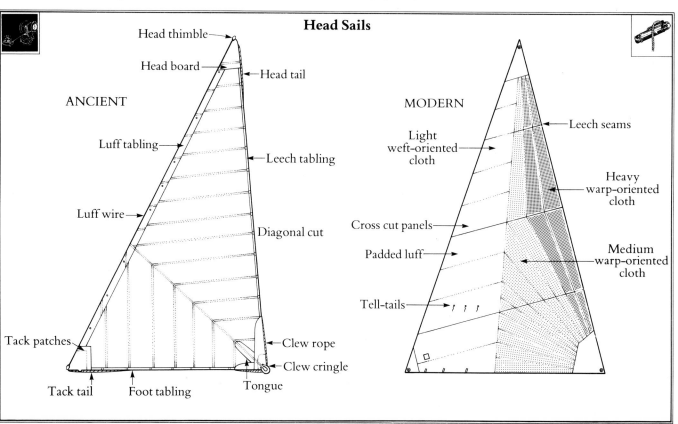

Head Sails

ANCIENT

Head thimble
Head board — Head tail
Luff tabling — Leech tabling
Luff wire
Diagonal cut
Tack patches — Clew rope
— Clew cringle
Tack tail   Foot tabling   Tongue

MODERN

Light weft-oriented cloth — Leech seams
Cross cut panels — Heavy warp-oriented cloth
Padded luff
Tell-tails — Medium warp-oriented cloth

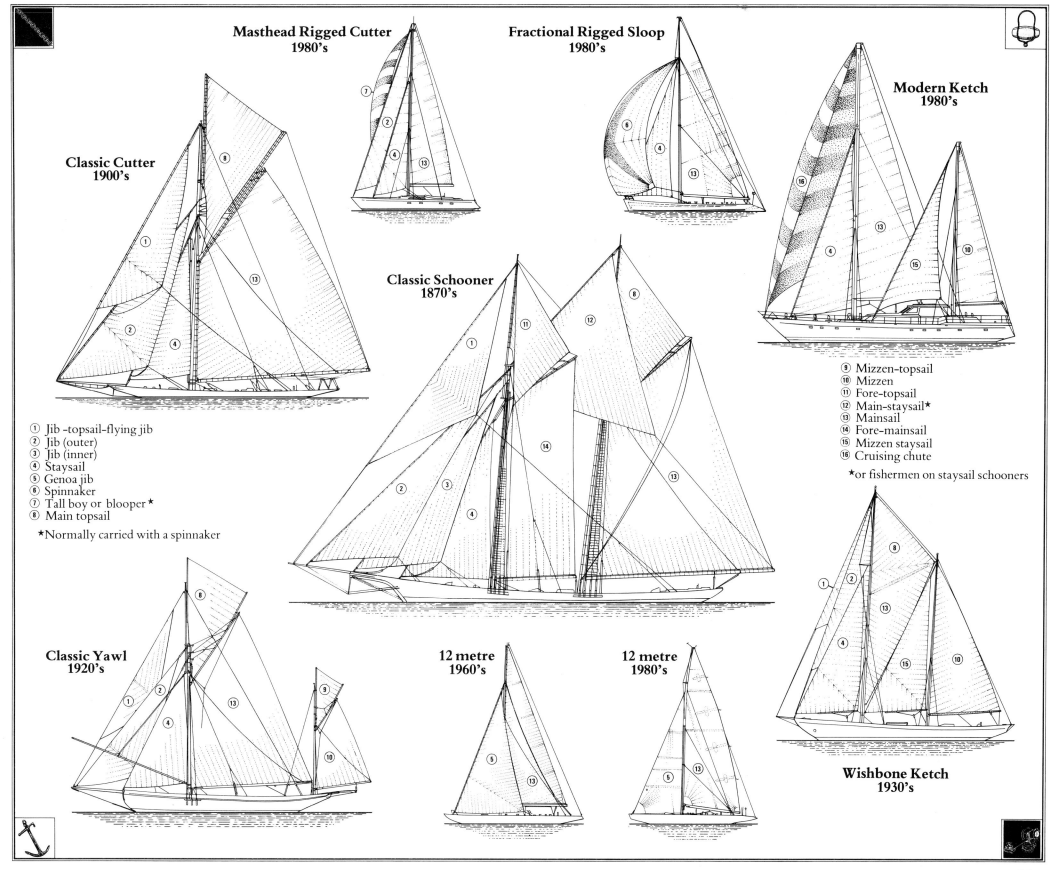

Masthead Rigged Cutter
1980's

Fractional Rigged Sloop
1980's

Modern Ketch
1980's

Classic Cutter
1900's

Classic Schooner
1870's

① Jib -topsail-flying jib
② Jib (outer)
③ Jib (inner)
④ Staysail
⑤ Genoa jib
⑥ Spinnaker
⑦ Tall boy or blooper ★
⑧ Main topsail

★Normally carried with a spinnaker

⑨ Mizzen-topsail
⑩ Mizzen
⑪ Fore-topsail
⑫ Main-staysail★
⑬ Mainsail
⑭ Fore-mainsail
⑮ Mizzen staysail
⑯ Cruising chute

★or fishermen on staysail schooners

Classic Yawl
1920's

12 metre
1960's

12 metre
1980's

Wishbone Ketch
1930's

RIGGING AND EQUIPMENT

A member of the famous Herreshoff family is once said to have stated that 'outside of a few exceptions, marine hardware is largely trash.' Today nothing could be further from the truth. New synthetic sail materials are now so immensely strong that in a blow they are often the last, no longer the first, to give in. It stands, therefore, that as yachts are driven harder, masts, rigging and most of a modern lady's equipment have to be very robust indeed.

It was not until the year 1858 that the solid wooden masts of pitch, Oregon or Norway pine, stepped in vessels since the beginning of sail, were changed for the first hollow mast, fitted to a British yacht called *Black Maria*. But the idea was treated with great suspicion until first Michael Ratsey lightened *Cambria*'s stick by boring 4in (100mm) diameter holes to meet from each end, and then Charles Nicholson in 1912 fitted *Shamrock IV*'s prototype *Istria* with his revolutionary hollow 'Marconi' topmast. The extruded light-alloy spars that we are now accustomed to, however, were originally the brainchild of Starling Burgess, designer of the 'tin mast' for the American yacht *Enterprise*, winner of the America's Cup in 1930.

By the turn of the twentieth century, although yachts were already using steel plough wire for stays and shrouds (it was long before the days of nylon or Dacron), either manila, hemp, coir or cotton rope, often led through a block and tackle, was always used for running rigging. Again it was the America's Cup which had the greatest influence on future materials, and in 1934 Frank Murdoch, Sopwith's technical adviser on *Endeavour*, and Starling Burgess on *Rainbow* separately developed steel, now streamlined-cobalt, rod rigging. Frank Murdoch had also specified every type of new gadget for *Endeavour*, including tension meters, speedometers, range finders and wind gauges, designed on many of the same principles used for yacht instruments today. But computers are now taking over fast.

Sails which once could only be changed or reefed with difficulty in a squall can now be shortened by hydraulics, sometimes the main being furled cleverly inside the boom or mast, and, with the advent of stronger synthetic rope, sail-handling gear has also experienced dramatic changes. The old two-geared steel winches first fitted on the later Js have since been replaced by reverse-action titanium self-tailers, which, in order to keep the crew in shape, are now often cross-linked for a little double-handed, multi-geared, high-speed coffee grinding.

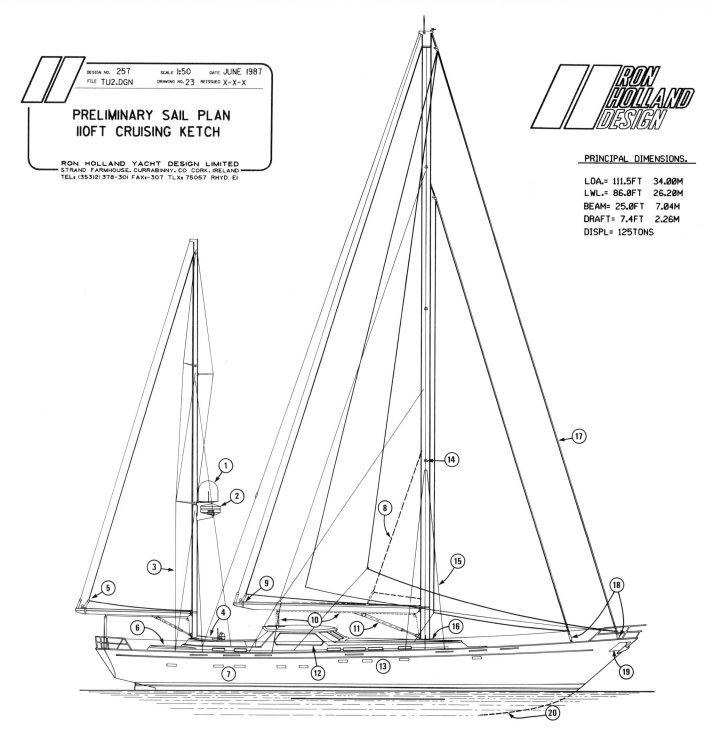

DESIGN NO. 257	SCALE 1:50	DATE JUNE 1987
FILE TU2.DGN	DRAWING NO. 23	REISSUED X-X-X

PRELIMINARY SAIL PLAN
110FT CRUISING KETCH

RON HOLLAND YACHT DESIGN LIMITED
STRAND FARMHOUSE. CURRABINNY. CO CORK. IRELAND
TEL: (353)21 378-301 FAX: -307 TLX: 75057 RHYD EI

RON HOLLAND DESIGN

PRINCIPAL DIMENSIONS.

LOA.= 111.5FT   34.00M
LWL.= 86.0FT   26.20M
BEAM= 25.0FT   7.04M
DRAFT= 7.4FT   2.26M
DISPL= 125TONS

① SATCOM for telephone communications
② Radar
③ Solid rod rigging
④ Helm station controls engines and under deck sheet winches
⑤ Hydraulic furling Mizzen
⑥ Under deck genoa sheet self stowing winches
⑦ Performance under power as good as displacement motor yachts. 13 Kts.

⑧ Hydraulic furling Mainsail
⑨ Outhaul (clew) hydraulically operated
⑩ Main sheet to under deck hydraulic self stowing winch
⑪ Hydraulic/air boom vang/strut
⑫ Inside control station
⑬ No ventilators on deck (air conditioning)
⑭ Three spreaders for maximum mast support

⑮ Solid rod rigging
⑯ Staysail sheet winches and main mast halyard winches self stowing (hydraulic) under flush deck hatches
⑰ 1 × 19 or 1 × 37 (32mm) headstay/backstay
⑱ Hydraulic roller furling
⑲ Recessed (under deck) anchor system
⑳ Hydraulic bow thruster (retractable)

Modern ketch

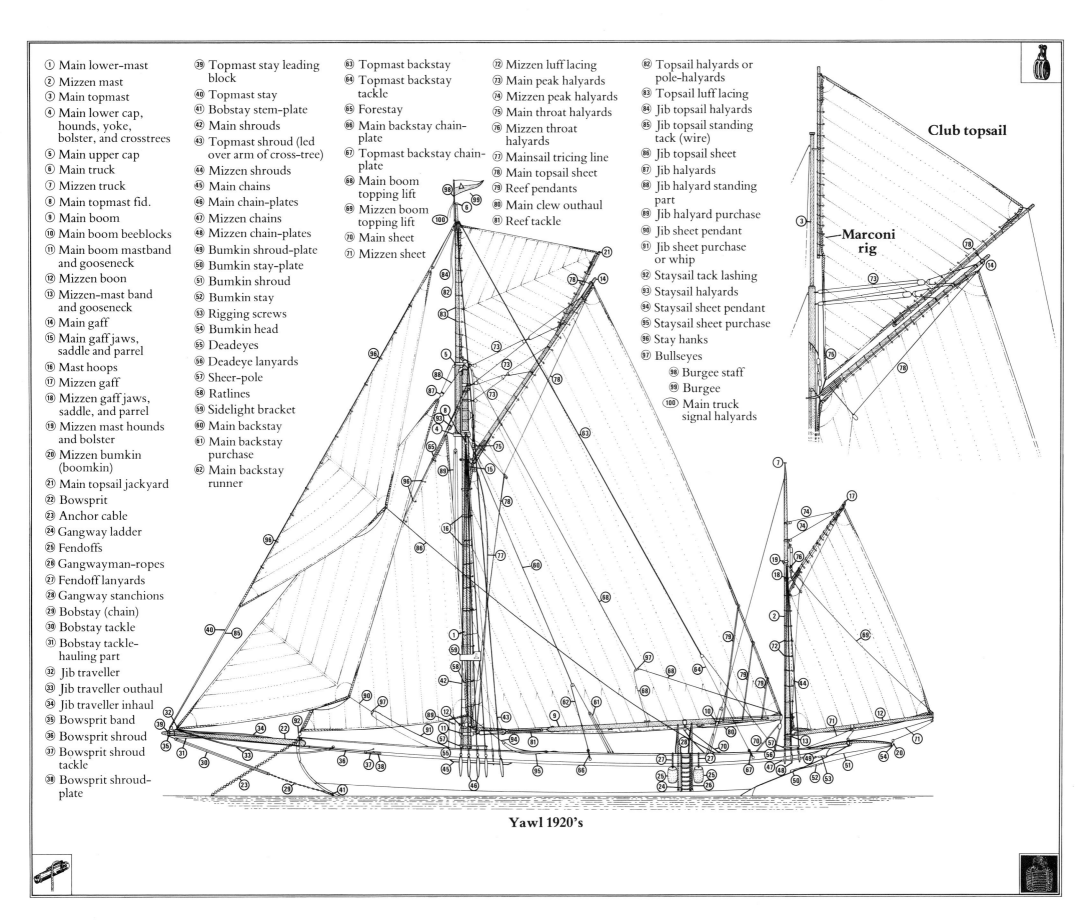

1 Main lower-mast
2 Mizzen mast
3 Main topmast
4 Main lower cap, hounds, yoke, bolster, and crosstrees
5 Main upper cap
6 Main truck
7 Mizzen truck
8 Main topmast fid.
9 Main boom
10 Main boom beeblocks
11 Main boom mastband and gooseneck
12 Mizzen boon
13 Mizzen-mast band and gooseneck
14 Main gaff
15 Main gaff jaws, saddle and parrel
16 Mast hoops
17 Mizzen gaff
18 Mizzen gaff jaws, saddle, and parrel
19 Mizzen mast hounds and bolster
20 Mizzen bumkin (boomkin)
21 Main topsail jackyard
22 Bowsprit
23 Anchor cable
24 Gangway ladder
25 Fendoffs
26 Gangwayman-ropes
27 Fendoff lanyards
28 Gangway stanchions
29 Bobstay (chain)
30 Bobstay tackle
31 Bobstay tackle-hauling part
32 Jib traveller
33 Jib traveller outhaul
34 Jib traveller inhaul
35 Bowsprit band
36 Bowsprit shroud
37 Bowsprit shroud tackle
38 Bowsprit shroud-plate

39 Topmast stay leading block
40 Topmast stay
41 Bobstay stem-plate
42 Main shrouds
43 Topmast shroud (led over arm of cross-tree)
44 Mizzen shrouds
45 Main chains
46 Main chain-plates
47 Mizzen chains
48 Mizzen chain-plates
49 Bumkin shroud-plate
50 Bumkin stay-plate
51 Bumkin shroud
52 Bumkin stay
53 Rigging screws
54 Bumkin head
55 Deadeyes
56 Deadeye lanyards
57 Sheer-pole
58 Ratlines
59 Sidelight bracket
60 Main backstay
61 Main backstay purchase
62 Main backstay runner

63 Topmast backstay
64 Topmast backstay tackle
65 Forestay
66 Main backstay chain-plate
67 Topmast backstay chain-plate
68 Main boom topping lift
69 Mizzen boom topping lift
70 Main sheet
71 Mizzen sheet

72 Mizzen luff lacing
73 Main peak halyards
74 Mizzen peak halyards
75 Main throat halyards
76 Mizzen throat halyards
77 Mainsail tricing line
78 Main topsail sheet
79 Reef pendants
80 Main clew outhaul
81 Reef tackle

82 Topsail halyards or pole-halyards
83 Topsail luff lacing
84 Jib topsail halyards
85 Jib topsail standing tack (wire)
86 Jib topsail sheet
87 Jib halyards
88 Jib halyard standing part
89 Jib halyard purchase
90 Jib sheet pendant
91 Jib sheet purchase or whip
92 Staysail tack lashing
93 Staysail halyards
94 Staysail sheet pendant
95 Staysail sheet purchase
96 Stay hanks
97 Bullseyes
98 Burgee staff
99 Burgee
100 Main truck signal halyards

Club topsail

Marconi rig

Yawl 1920's

Classic yawl

THE OWNERS
AND THEIR CREWS

Sir Robert he stood beside me as I worked her down to
    the mark;
'There's money on this, my lad,' said he, 'and most
    of 'em's running dark;
But ease the sheet if you're bunkered, and back the
    scrimmages tight,
And use your slide at the distance, and we'll drink
    to your health tonight!'

From the ballad of the *Jubilee Cup*
by Sir A. Quiller-Couch

Not all of 'em who owned the great yachts of the past
were great yachtsmen. Sir Thomas Lipton in over
thirty years of indulging in his 'principle recreation'
seldom set foot on the deck of any of his six *Shamrocks*.
Others who were great yachtsmen, like Sir Thomas
Brassey, sometimes got short shrift in any case. 'I wish
the old bastard was up 'ere 'isself', complained a sailor
high in the rigging of his yacht *Sunbeam*. To which, so
the story goes, elderly Sir Thomas replied, 'the old
bastard *is* up here.' Even on motor yachts the nobs
were inclined to make the odd blunder, and when the
captain of one handsome ship rang down, 'finished
with engines', explaining to the noble peer who was
buying her, 'you could never do that with steam', he
replied, 'but isn't she steam Captain?' However, without such moneyed gentlemen prepared to gamble vast
sums on success or total failure, such as Thomas
Lawson who in 1901 spent the then vast sum of
$200,000 on building the hopeless America's Cup con-
tender *Independence* only to see her scrapped, the
world of yachting would have remained remarkably
small.

Fortunately such larger-than-life characters are still
around, and although much of the money they sub-
scribe comes through tax-efficient funds or corpora-
tions, maxi-yachts do get built as do the proliferation
of contenders for the now mega-million-dollar
America's Cup. Today, remarkably, there could be
over a hundred vessels of over 100ft (30m) on the
stocks of the world's boat yards at any one time, and
one, the 482ft (147m) *Abdul Aziz*, commissioned by
the King of Saudi Arabia and perhaps the most expensive private yacht ever built, is believed to have cost,
including her arsenal of guided missiles and a twenty-
seat helicopter, well over $100,000,000.

It would be interesting to draw a graph, if it hasn't
been done already, comparing the total value of the
world's yachts through the ages with the costs of running them. Again only yachts of over 50ft (15m) would

qualify, for there has been such growth in the small
boat market in recent years that the result would otherwise be distorted. Certainly history would prove that
yachting is not so much a sport, rather more a very expensive fashion, and apart from the famous owners,
like Sir Thomas (Tommy) Sopwith and Harold (Mike)
Vanderbilt, who skilfully helmed their yachts as
national heroes, there have been many more content,
as the owner of a runner at Ascot may be content, to
see their steeds being steered professionally while
grandly flying their racing colours.

Although there have always been professionals in all
types of yachting, most of the best remembered racing
skippers had made their mark long before the outbreak
of World War I. In America many of these tough
characters came from the oystering villages of Long
Island Sound or in southern New England or from
along the coast of Maine, while in Great Britain they
were more likely to have grown up on the Clyde, or in
the seaside villages of Essex, the fishing ports of the
Solent or further west in Torbay. The dashing Captain
Edward Sycamore, who came from Brightlingsea in
Essex and skippered many great yachts including
Shamrock (the 23 Metre) and the German-owned
Navahœ, had nerves of steel and was, as Nicholson put
it, as cunning as a fox. He would bemuse his opponents
into making the most embarrassing mistakes, but then,
having carved a path through most of the regatta season, he would spend the winter like so many of his contemporaries quietly inshore fishing off his favourite
Essex coast. The captains were always in sole command of their yachts and bore enormous responsi-
bility. Sometimes however, a yacht would carry a pilot
as *America* did when she came to England in 1851 to
guide her through the treacherous tides and shallows
of the Solent.

In the 1890s, probably the heyday of the famous professional skippers such as Hank Haff, William Cranfield, Archie Hogarth and Captain 'Cook' Diaper, there were probably more employed in the 'Big Class' alone than are employed in the whole yachting scene as we know it today. Working for less than £5 per week, sometimes with a winter retainer thrown in, they led a meagre lifestyle, often having to depend on winning races to supplement their pay.

It was not until 1913, after many professionals had been enticed away to Germany, that first in America, and then in Europe, amateur skippers began to take over. Such 'pier-head-jumpers' were not initially very popular, but some, such as Sir William Burton, who with *Shamrock IV* in 1920 came the closest yet to winning the America's Cup, and later Sir Philip Hunloke, master of the King's yacht *Britannia*, became formidable and much respected sailors.

Professional crew members in the 1890s were lucky if they earned more than £1 5s a week. Usually in their early twenties they had to be fit and young enough to keep to a rigorous routine throughout the summer and strong enough, before the advent of winches, to sweat in the heaviest sails. Discipline was strict, and often the crew were only allowed to use the precarious bowsprit, and not the gangway, when they had been ashore for a beer. Danger money was usually awarded for working aloft, sometimes at more than 150ft (46m) above the heaving deck, the only other perks being a possible 3s per week for good conduct and a few coins from the skipper's purse if the yacht was winning races.

From 1900 an increasing number of Scandinavians were being signed on, particularly by American owners, and in 1903 the America's Cup defender *Reliance* included many Scandinavians among her record complement of seventy crew. Although this was a stagger-

ing number of hands, crews of thirty-five to forty were not uncommon, and these were only reduced in size during the 1920s due to the easier handling characteristics of the new Bermudian sail. By the 1930s, crew wages had doubled to approximately £3 per week, thirty men still being required to handle a 'J', and by the 1980s to the daunting figure of £80,000 per year for a top skipper, or for an experienced crew member not less than £20 per day. But it is interesting that when in 1970 John Nicholson of Camper & Nicholson wrote in his book *Great Years in Yachting*, 'If some madman elected to build a J class cutter now, he could never find a professional crew', the way that the America's Cup is developing, he could, surprisingly, have been asked to eat his words.

The crew of the *Dauntless*

THE FUTURE

The correct definition of a yacht, some say, is a hole in the water surrounded by wood – or glass – or carbon-fibre – or any other space-age material that makes pouring money through it that much easier. Yachts are now becoming so sophisticated that it is surprising that anyone can afford one at all. But many people will. Not just to sail faster, look prettier or to catch the girls, but often to have a yacht that is a little more innovative, if only one step forward.

New synthetic materials no doubt will continue to have the greatest influence on future yacht design and as sails become almost indestructible the spars and handling equipment must themselves continue to improve. But it is probably in the sphere of communications and navigational equipment that the greatest advances will be made, and as satellite aerials become produced in miniature even the small cruising boat owner will be able to stow away his log and sextant and steer by computer – perhaps from home!

As the designers of racing yachts continue to find ways of exploiting the International Offshore Rule, new outlandish looking yachts will take to the water, none more sensational than the born again ninety-footers. Their deep keels and immense rigs at first seem a step back to the 1930's, but not in terms of performance. Masts are now made of carbon-fibre and titanium with rod rigging of lenticular cobalt steel, and such is likely to be the beam of these leviathans that the rig, mounted on the widest base, is unlikely to collapse in all but the mightiest blow. Some old salts would complain that playing the high-stakes, high-technology game makes yacht racing no longer a sport, but others like the notorious Earl of Dunraven would no doubt be there again – up to every trick in the book!

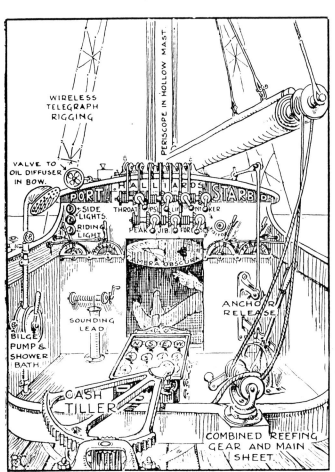

A boat of quiet habits (from *Yachting World*, c1920)

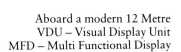

Aboard a modern 12 Metre
VDU – Visual Display Unit
MFD – Multi Functional Display

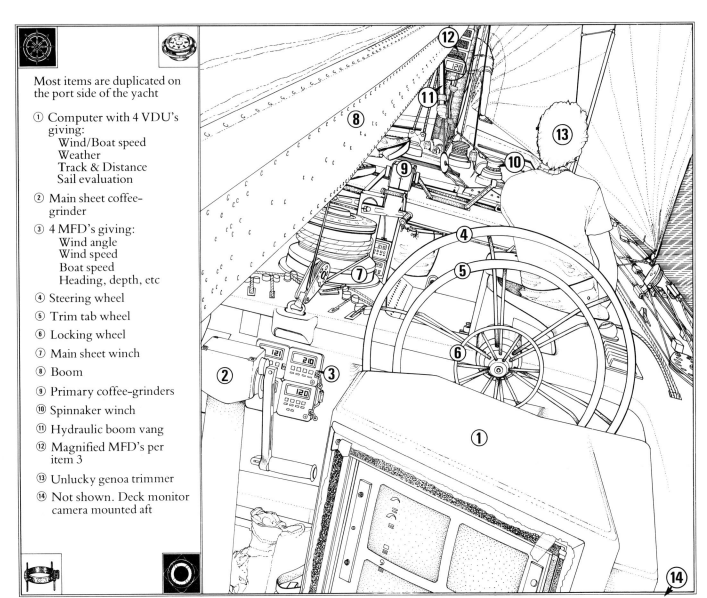

Most items are duplicated on the port side of the yacht

① Computer with 4 VDU's giving:
    Wind/Boat speed
    Weather
    Track & Distance
    Sail evaluation

② Main sheet coffee-grinder

③ 4 MFD's giving:
    Wind angle
    Wind speed
    Boat speed
    Heading, depth, etc

④ Steering wheel

⑤ Trim tab wheel

⑥ Locking wheel

⑦ Main sheet winch

⑧ Boom

⑨ Primary coffee-grinders

⑩ Spinnaker winch

⑪ Hydraulic boom vang

⑫ Magnified MFD's per item 3

⑬ Unlucky genoa trimmer

⑭ Not shown. Deck monitor camera mounted aft

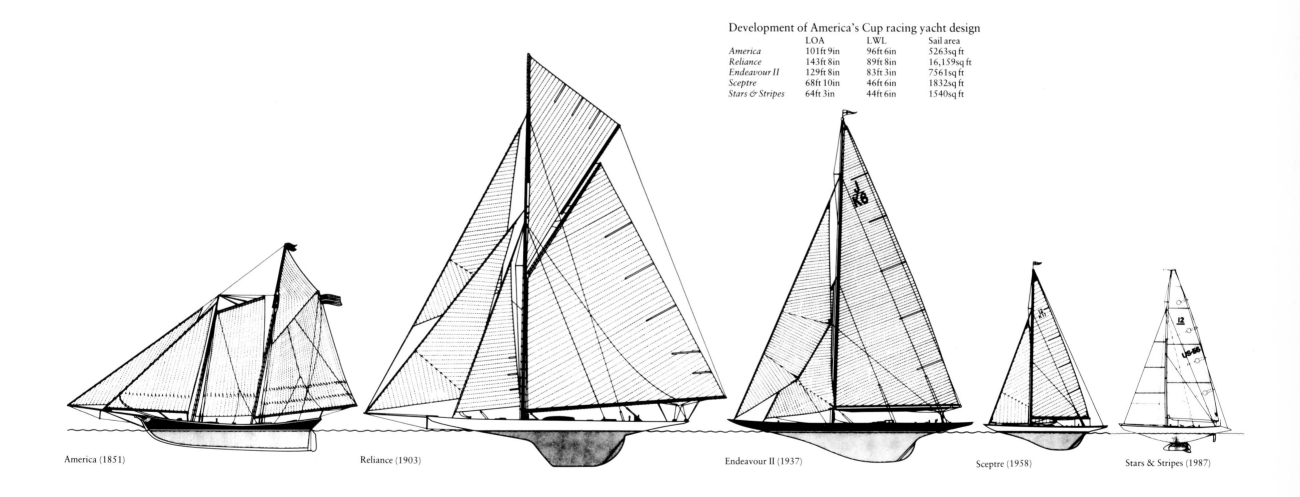

Development of America's Cup racing yacht design

	LOA	LWL	Sail area
America	101ft 9in	96ft 6in	5263sq ft
Reliance	143ft 8in	89ft 8in	16,159sq ft
Endeavour II	129ft 8in	83ft 3in	7561sq ft
Sceptre	68ft 10in	46ft 6in	1832sq ft
Stars & Stripes	64ft 3in	44ft 6in	1540sq ft

America (1851)

Reliance (1903)

Endeavour II (1937)

Sceptre (1958)

Stars & Stripes (1987)

'PEARL'   THE 'FALCON'   'WATERWITCH'

351 *tons (Earl of Yarborough)*

Off Spithead with the Royal Yacht Squadron on their voyage to Cherbourg, 1832

CHRONOLOGY OF YACHTING

1551 The word yacht first appears in the *Histoire de la Marine Française.*

1660 King Charles II lands in England by yacht from Holland.
The *Mary*, England's first yacht, is presented by the Dutch.

1661 The first yacht race between the yachts of the King and the Duke of York, from Greenwich to Gravesend and back on the River Thames.

1675 First known account of yacht cruising.

1720 Water Club of Cork Harbour – the world's first yacht club conducted the first known regatta.

1770 The first British yacht club founded at Starcross in Devon.

1775 Formation of the Cumberland Fleet on the Thames.
The first English yacht race for other than royalty, from Westminster Bridge to Putney Bridge and back.

1776 The first sailing match outside the Thames, a regatta at Cowes, Isle of Wight.

1815 Founding of The Yacht Club at Cowes, Isle of Wight, re-named in 1833 The Royal Yacht Squadron.

1829 The first handicap race for yachts based on time allowance organised by The Royal Yacht Squadron at Cowes.

1835 The first yacht race in America, rounding Cape Cod.

1844 Foundation of The New York Yacht Club, the first yacht club in the United States of America.

1844 The first New York Yacht Club Cruise.

1849 The first international yacht race ever sailed. Held in Bermuda.

1851 Race at Cowes for the 100 Guineas Cup, later to become The America's Cup.

1853 Vanderbilt's *North Star* is launched, the first steam yacht in America.

1866 The first transatlantic race (held from west to east).

1875 Formation of The Yacht Racing Association. Since 1953 known as The Royal Yachting Association, RYA.

1876 The yacht *Sunbeam* cruises around the world.

1893 The era of the big boat class begins with the launching of *Britannia* and many other great racing cutters.

1897 Inauguration of the North American Yacht Racing Union in New York.

1898 Joshua Slocum becomes the first man to circumnavigate the world alone.

1899 The first of Lipton's famous *Shamrock*s challenges for The America's Cup.

1900 Yacht racing first included in the Olympic Games held in France.

1903 *Reliance*, the largest racing cutter ever, is launched.

1906 First ocean race from the United States to Bermuda. The yacht *Atlantic* sets up the transatlantic record for monohulls.

1907 The International Yacht Racing Union, IYRU, formed at a conference held in Paris.

1925 The first Fastnet race starting at Ryde, Isle of Wight, and finishing at Plymouth with the formation of The Ocean Racing Club.

1937 *Ranger* wins the last America's Cup raced by 'J' class yachts.

1941 The first Southern Ocean Racing Conference, SORC series (Florida).

1945 The first Sydney to Hobart race, now the most important ocean race in the Southern Hemisphere.

1957 The first inshore/offshore series – named The Admiral's Cup.

1958 The first 12 Metres race for The America's Cup.

1962 The first challenge by Australia for The America's Cup.

1967 Francis Chichester returns from his one-stop circumnavigation.

1968 Bernard Moitessier sets out on a non-stop single-handed passage one and a half times round the world.

1969 Robin Knox-Johnston becomes the first man to sail solo round the world without stopping.

1970 The International Offshore Rule adopted for yacht racing worldwide.

1974 The first round-the-world race for fully crewed yachts.

1983 The New York Yacht Club loses The America's Cup after 132 years (won by *Australia II*).

1987 The America's Cup regained by the United States (*Stars & Stripes*).

1988 New Zealand challenges for The America's Cup with a ninety-footer.

DETAILS OF THE PAINTINGS

Tim Thompson's paintings, featured in this book, are
as follows:

Enquiries about paintings still on exhibition, or about reproductions, may be made to:
Tim Thompson, Ashcombe Tower, Dawlish, Devon, England.

ACKNOWLEDGEMENTS

My first thanks go to the Royal Yacht Squadron and to their secretary Robin Rising for their invaluable and enthusiastic support in allowing me to once again invade the privacy of their splendid library. Also I would like to thank the New York Yacht Club, in particular their librarian Mr Hohri for researching many obscure details long embedded in their copious filing system. Bob Ward at the Royal Thames Yacht Club has been especially helpful, for which I am greatly indebted, as have the Royal Torbay Yacht Club and the Royal Cruising Club in London.

The National Maritime Museum have assisted me considerably as have Mystic Seaport Museum in Connecticut and the Museum of Yachting, Newport, Rhode Island. I would also like to thank Joe Gribbins of *Nautical Quarterly* magazine in the United States.

Many of the writers that have contributed to *The Story of Yachting* are now sadly 'at anchor', but of those who are still at full sail I should particularly like to mention Ian Dear, author of *Enterprise to Endeavour*, *The America's Cup: an Informal History* and *Fastnet: the Story of a Great Ocean Race*. Also John Rousmaniere, author of *The America's Cup 1851–1983* and *The Golden Pastime*, and Bruce Stannard who wrote *Ben Lexcen, the Man, the Keel and the Cup*.

Both Nigel Irens and Ron Holland, two of the world's leading yacht designers, have been extremely generous in sending me plans of some of their most recent creations, and I would like to thank Nigel Burgess, Messrs Camper & Nicholsons and Rosie for providing me with information on several yachts at present in commission.

Finally I am grateful to my secretary Jackie Colquhoun, who has so beautifully executed the pencil portraits for the book, to Ethan Danielson for his superb line drawings and to my wife Annette, who has helped me with the text. But above all my thanks go to Tim Thompson for his untiring efforts in producing some of the most magnificent marine paintings I have ever seen and for the support given him by his family.